BLACKSMITH TO BRIEFCASE

The Author's Grandchildren

From left to right – Tom Jones, Robert Strange, Emily Strange, Joseph Jones, Helen Strange, David Strange.

Blacksmith

to

Briefcase

Alf Strange

Robert R Muller

Gee & Son Limited
Denbigh

First Impression: May 2000

ISBN 0 7074 0335 9

By the same author:

Me Dad's the Village Blacksmith
Following Me Dad
Forging Ahead

Cover and Frontispiece photographs by "Take Two Photography", Malpas.

Printed and Published by:
GEE & SON (DENBIGH) LTD.
NORTH WALES LL16 3SW

About the Author

Alf Strange became well known in 1925 – just after his Mother Emily had finished walking up the stairs backwards, in the hope that her fourth child would be a "Freda" – but alas she got an "Alfred". But it was in the border and lovely village of Welsh Frankton that anybody knew of him, - and more particularly in the hamlet of the Perthy a "suburb" of Welsh Frankton, everybody knew everything in the Perthy.

However "The Stranges" were important people for "Me Dad's the Village Blacksmith". The Village Blacksmith was unofficially elected by popular acclaim as 'Village First Citizen'.

Soon Alf became known in the nearby lovely mere town of Ellesmere; just as soon as he could kick a football, and hit a cricket ball far and often 'wide'.

Since the eighties knowledge of Alf has spread afar. Following a serious illness Alf became the first Blacksmith to turn to the pen for non technical subjects. He wrote the popular book "Me Dad's the Village Blacksmith" It has sold thousands of copies. But Alf did not benefit financially from this achievement he chose to give all the profits to Copthorne Hospital, now known as The Royal Shrewsbury Hospital. To date he has handed over in the region of £9,000.

He has been heard many times on the Radio and has appeared on television. Alf now travels the West Midlands giving talks – and he is just at home in front of a group of Village Womens Institute members as he is chatting to a large group of professional people in the City of Birmingham.

In 1986 a second book came off the press – "Following me Dad". That book starts where the first book finished, at the outbreak of the 1939-45 war, and goes to the early fifties. His books are to be found in Somerset, Wiltshire, London, Cumbria, Leicestershire, Nottingham, Australia and America.

He has collected tools and equipment used by the blacksmith who up until 1947 were ageless in his work. He has opened a museum to the public. He demonstrates the art and skill and talks all the time he is doing so about "The Village Blacksmith". To date thousands of people have watched and listened to him. Alf is a qualified and expert farrier (he spent the war 'under a horse'). His knowledge on the history of horseshoes and on horses feet is second to none. He is in possession of a horseshoe that is believed to be 300 years old.

The old farmhouse where Alf and his wife Vera live was once a public house called "The Green Man" and was regularly visited by 'Mad Jack Mytton'. Nowadays visitors can still see the escape tunnel that Jack used when the Peelers raided the cock-fighting pit at the back of the pub.

A third book followed, "Forging Ahead", and Alf's latest book "Blacksmith to Briefcase" will be released shortly, but if you do get the chance to see or hear Alf then take a handkerchief with you as tears of laughter will soon flow.

Alf's books are suitable for all, from 9 to 90 !!!!!

BERNARD HALLETT

Publishers' Note: The author of the above article sadly passed away before this book was completed.

ACKNOWLEDGEMENTS

Again I wish to record sincere thanks to my friend, Mr. Iorwerth Roberts for his invaluable assistance during the preparation of this book.

My thanks also are due once again to the publishers, Gee and Son (Denbigh) Ltd., for all their help and guidance.

Contents

THE DEMISE OF A VILLAGE 9
THE PROBLEMS OF A PUBLIC SPEAKER 12
EVERGREEN EVENING 17
A VOICE FROM THE PAST 20
A PIKEL'S TALE 21
DATES I WILL ALWAYS REMEMBER 22
THE ELLESMERE EXHIBITION OF 1982 31
THE MOMENT OF TRUTH 34
THE DIVA AND THE ANVIL CHORUS 36
LAMB CHOPS FOR LUCK 37
A SAD DAY AT LLANGOLLEN 39
OUTSIDE LOO 40
SMITHY AND FARM MUSEUM 44
THE VICAR'S FAREWELL 45
BLACKSMITH TURNED ACTOR 47
END OF AN ERA 52
ABSENT FRIENDS – 1946-99 54
THE REVEREND AND THE MOTHERS' UNION 57
STICKY END 58
NO NEED FOR MY FERTILE HORSESHOE! 59
THE OFFER OF A JOB 61
FRED GREGORY 65
SEQUEL TO A QUIET PINT 68
A VISIT FROM SOME AMERICAN FRIENDS 70
LOOK AFTER YOURSELF 72
COUNTRY EDUCATION TO THE FORE 74
LLANGOLLEN EISTEDDFOD 76
HERE FOR THE DAY 81
TO DRINK OR NOT TO DRINK 83
PANIC STATIONS!!! 84
METRES OF CONCRETE 86
BRISTOL CRAWLER? – NO FRANKTON PLODDER!! 87
A PERSIAN CAT FROM CREWE 89

How long in the public eye? 91
Clayton Jones – poet 92
The building up of a museum 96
Gooseberries and custard!! 99
Fenn's bank last turf barrow 100
Mast foreman – Girl of 25 102
Take not the life you can give, because everything
    has a right to live! 104
Late night shopping has a twist! 107
The olympic games – 1948 108
The day we nearly held up royalty 109
Oh no! royalty again 111
The church and school at welsh frankton 113
Alf strange – blacksmith 114
My life (by a railway container) 115
Mr Grafton Beddows 120
A fanatical liverpool supporter 120
A feed of fish and chips – for two 121
A night to remember 122
Life can be so cruel 124
To rescue a chicken or save a life 127
A dog's life 128
A domineering woman in the party 130
Deaf people at the back of the room 131
A wet saturday morning in april 1995 133
The salters of stanham 135
The salters of america 139
A visit from the children of chernobyl 146
A little bit of advice 148
The dolls houses find a new home 149
Oh be thankful, count your blessings, oh be grateful 151
Don't give up 152
Farewell bernard 153
Excitement at babbinswood 154
The sequel – sixty years on 155
A fast stretch of road 156
A sad day at cloy hall 157
Letters 159
The final chapter 166

"The Demise of a Village"

In this my fourth and final book I start the first chapter with the single word "GONE" and the changes I have seen in my 74 years of living in our little village of Welsh Frankton.

"GONE" is the village shop where our 'penny' on a Saturday night would buy us lads 2 sticks of Spanish Juice and 22 aniseed balls or 21 peppermints to suck in chapel on a Sunday morning. If you dropped an aniseed ball it would bounce across the wooden chapel floor, one dare not look at my Mother's face because the saying 'if looks could kill' rang very true whenever that happened.

"GONE" are Mrs Beckit and Miss King who used to serve such things as paraffin in there. They would weigh out chicken corn at so much a pound out of a sack into a brown paper bag with the aid of a steel scoop. No special offers in those days! The price of food, for example, cheese, sugar, jam, bread very rarely altered from one year to the next. We used to fetch 10 Woodbines for a chap called Jack Reeves, payment for that would be a 'fag' between two of you. The smell of soft soap and different kinds of food and other goods mingled together to create a smell one cannot describe. The Ministry of Health would not have a book big enough to record the breach of health regulations, especially when occasionally the odd mouse would jump out of a sack of chicken corn, but somehow we survived!

"GONE" are Mrs Hayward, Mrs Walter Jones and Mrs Colesby who lived in Bottle Row, the row of houses opposite the school. They would make you a cup of cocoa for a halfpenny at dinnertime, five cups for 2½d per week, very much appreciated on a cold wet day in winter.

"GONE" is the old school, made into an engineering works which exports parts and water tanks all over the world, and in one room a fax machine and a mobile phone is a must. Gone is the old fireplace in which Mrs. Jeffreys tragically lost her life, it has made way for a block of toilets – flush toilets! What were they?

"GONE" also is the railway station, from where one could travel to Oswestry or Ellesmere for only a few pence and make connections to anywhere in the country.

"GONE" too is Tom Hyde's bus which also did a twice weekly run to Oswestry and Ellesmere. It was famous for the yearly run to New Brighton, 3 hours by bus, the modern car would take about 50 minutes, but are we happy?

"GONE" also is the puff and energy that the writer of these words had when he used to run all the way from home to school at the tender age of $3\frac{1}{2}$!!

"GONE" also is the petrol station built some 30 odd years ago. What a revelation that was, petrol in our own little village. Gone – a sign of the economic climate.

"GONE" quite recently, in fact, the village Post Office on the retirement of Grace Ankers who has served all and sundry for the last 27 years, as well as rearing a family of seven and six grandchildren. How she finds time to play a round of golf at her local club The Brow Golf Club as well as looking after her husband Tony I will never know!

So now the writer of these words who first went into the Post Office some 70 odd years ago will have to get his bike out and cycle to Ellesmere to collect his pension, and hopefully not get mugged on the way home. I say the word bike as with petrol prices rising at the rate they are I will not be able to afford to get my 18-year old car out of the garage to fetch my pension. It just will not be worth it.

Still going and holding regular services are The United Reformed Church and The Church of England, although numbers are well down on what they used to be when both were built some 160 years ago, but what was a car park then!

Still going strong is the Parish Hall, with its weekly table tennis matches and also line dancing, who would have thought of it in 1928 when the hall was first open and the rule was that No Alcohol was to be consumed on the premises. What was a can of beer then?

As strong as ever are the monthly meetings of the local W.I. now in their 70th year. They are no longer 'Jam and Jerusalem' and have been known to sway governments, certainly local governments. Mention the words Women's Institute and knees begin to tremble.

Welsh Frankton has a thriving Women Institute with its President being Mrs Carol Jones, Secretary: Mrs Barbara Smith, Treasurer: Mrs Heather Elder and Press Secretary: Mrs Isabel Jones.

Another group still going strong is our local Mother's Union well managed by Enrolling Member: Mrs Marie Powell, Secretary: Mrs. E. Pritchard, Treasurer: Mrs. Rosemary Powell, and Press Secretary: Mrs. Debbie Hayward.

Although only a few in number their Annual Garden Fete in Marie's garden is a must, and I was there the night Wal's very strong carrot wine got mixed up with the not so strong wine, and a good time was had by all!!

A reconstruction of a 300 year old smithy at the museum at Brow Farm.

The Problems of a Public Speaker

A letter arrives to say 'We are making our programme up for next year and your name has been given to us as a speaker'. The date we have available is Feb 30th.'

With a bit of luck there is a telephone number, but not always.

I telephone the writer and a definite date is fixed for me to visit them one evening the following winter (I only go out to speak from October till March as I am too busy in the summer doing Blacksmith Demonstrations).

"I will telephone you a few days before you are coming to make sure you are still alive!" Some bookings can be as far ahead as 2 years.

A few days before the appointed date I receive a telephone call to say we are looking forward to your talk on such and such an evening, - and I then ask "What time do you want me to speak?"

"Well the meeting starts at half past seven."

"Yes" I say "but what time do you want me to speak?"

"Well we will say 8 o'clock, all the business will be done by then" (I have heard those words many times.)

"Oh, and could you save me a car space please." I say.

"Oh yes, we always leave the speaker a car space."

So it is all arranged, 8 o'clock speaking and a car space- as you have done about another 50 times with many other W.I. meetings, nothing could possibly go wrong, or so you think!

Come the appointed night, away you go. As usual it is raining or snowing, you arrive at the Parish Hall at about quarter to eight – but alas, no car space, the car park full. In a space reserved for me I find an old Land Rover parked with possibly a dead sheep in the back with worm drench bottles and an empty syringe. At least, you know there is at least one farmer's wife there.

You peep through the curtains to see if the President is wearing a hat, if she is you know that she is the boss for the night. You open the door to the Parish Hall making sure that you make as much noise as you can to let her (The President I mean) know that you have arrived and you give her a wave.

The rest of the W.I. ladies know you have arrived because they all turn around to have a look at you. Then the speaker's host for the evening will come down the room to meet you.

"You're wet, Mr Strange," she will say. You try to explain to her that you could not get on the car park due to a clapped out old Land Rover with a dead sheep in the back.

At this she will point out that the lady whose husband owns the Land Rover – and the dead sheep has done this before, many times! She is always late because she has been helping her husband calve a cow or lamb some old ewes.

The president has told her off many times about this but she is such a good member and we don't want to lose her because we have a fete at their farm every year and she also gives the milk for our cup of tea and also for another 'do' that is held in the Parish Hall, she is so good hearted.

So we, the Speaker's Hostess and I sit down in the back row. I give a quick glance at my watch, just gone 8 o'clock. I try to fathom out how far the President has got with the meeting hoping that she has at least read the news letter, but alas, no, she has just picked it up out of her big pile of papers.

A wonderful letter is the newsletter, it covers everything from pieces of poetry to cures for everything and bits about other events etc. etc. She reads about three or four items out of it the fact that you have heard them the previous night does not matter to her. By now it is ten past eight.

Where-ever you go someone knows someone from Welsh Frankton – a wonderful village is Welsh Frankton. Your hostess wakes you up by saying that she knew Hilda Jones who was born on the Perthy, married Bill Hall.

13

"Do you know her, Mr Strange?"

"Yes" I said "I have known Hilda all my life, she is a great-grandmother you know."

"Never" says my hostess, "How old is she?"

"82," I say, "and still riding her new bike that her daughters bought for her 80th birthday".

Or you might get somebody say "Do you know Tommy Gardner?"

"Yes I know Tommy Gardner," I say, "I play golf with Tommy."

"He taught me to play golf" she will say, "such patience" Or another might say "Do you know Derek Wiggins? I went to school with him, he was a rum lad in his school days," and so it goes on.

"Norman Birch out of the co-op" one would say "and Walter Vickers who married Beryl Bowen from Welshampton."

According to what part of the country you are speaking, you can well depend someone will know someone from Welsh Frankton.

Only last year on a couple of days break in the Lake District at Lake Windermere a voice said "What are you doing up here?" It was a lady from Ellesmere, two miles from where I live visiting her daughter who lives up there.

By now it is 20 past 8 and the lady who went to the A.G.M. in London is going to tell everyone in detail about her trip to the A.G.M. You can tell she was the London delegate because she had freshly permed hair and is wearing a nice new dress.

"Could you make it brief," says the President to her.

But no, this is her night and she is going to make the most of it. I have heard more talks about the A.G.M. than any other man in the country. On she rambles. By now my hostess is getting a bit edgy, we have run out of conversation , so she starts to think of excuses for the other.

"We were a bit late starting to-night, Mrs so-an-so who always opens up the Hall and switches on the heaters was a bit late getting here with the key. She had been to her

14

daughter-in-law's for the day and the bus was a bit late getting her back, so we couldn't get into the hall at 7.15."

"It can't be helped" I say, glancing again at my watch at 8.30.

Suddenly the London delegate is nearly finished, but she has just a few more words to say about how some of the delegates went to meet Princess Diana after the meeting and goes on to say what a charming girl she is.

My hostess whispers to me that she has no time for Prince Charles and what ever he sees in Camilla Parker-Bowles she will never know.

I agree with her because I realise it won't be long before I start speaking and I wish I had not had that extra cup of coffee at tea-time.

I decide to pop into the toilet. I know it is the toilet because it had toilet written on the door. I was just about to open the door when a voice said "there is no bulb in the gent's toilet" I stop and someone laughingly says "Has any one got a torch he could borrow?" Someone else says "If there is no one in the ladies he can go in there." I wait for a few seconds to make sure all the ladies are present in the main room.

Arriving back the hostess proceeds to tell me about her husband who is waiting for his operation as he sometimes has to go to the loo 8 or 9 times in the night.

The President has finished and is about to welcome me to speak when in a loud voice she says: "any other business" I have already said a prayer to the Almighty saying "Please Jesus, don't let there be any other business."

But no, a little old lady on my left puts her hand up and says "Why are we going to Bodnant Gardens again? We went there 2 years ago and it rained all day."

"Well," said the President, "it was passed unanimously at the last meeting". "I know," says Penelope "but I was not at the last meeting. I was baby sitting for my daughter and son-in-law, they have four children you know, and it was the only night they had out together for years, they went to see Daniel O'Donnell and I did ask Mrs Hughes to say that I wanted to

15

go to Chatsworth House in Derbyshire because my sister lives near there and was going to join us there."

"Well," the President says, "I am sorry but our outing secretary has great difficulty trying to please everyone."

By now I know who the outing secretary is. She is sitting just two rows in front of me, a little to the left. She is the lady whose neck is beginning to go red and you just know that any minute she could explode – and she does. She suddenly gets up with her bundles of notes, marches up to the President's table bangs them down onto the table, turns to poor Penelope and says: "If you can do the job any better you can have a go. I've done it for 5 years and all I get if it is a wet day it is my fault, so here you have a go, because I am sick up to here with the job," and she puts her hand up to her chin.

By now everyone is having a free for all. The President's bell is ringing like mad, but no one takes any notice. Things are being said which would be better not said.

Suddenly the President shouts "Shut Up, Whatever will Mr Strange think of us."

The fact is that I have probably witnessed the same thing happening twenty times in the last six months, so I think it is just part of belonging to the W.I. movement. I Love You All!!!!.

By now it is about 20 to 9 and I start my talk by saying: "Perhaps, Madam President you will let me know did you go to Bodnant Gardens or not?

Evergreen Evening

One winter's evening in February I answered the telephone to be greeted by a dear old Welsh Lady saying in a loud voice "Is that Mr. Strange?" (Welsh ladies who are getting on a bit usually do shout down the phone).

"This is Mr. Strange" I said, to this she replied: "Mr. Strange can you come and give us a talk?"

"When did you have in mind." I enquired,

"Can you come next Tuesday?" she asked.

"I am very sorry," I replied, "But the earliest I can speak to you or any other group is October."

"Oh" she said, "It is eight months till October."

"Yes" I said, "But October will soon come, give me your name and telephone number and how many are in your group."

I will never forget her reply as long as I live.

She said "We call ourselves The Evergreens; we are all getting on a bit, there are thirteen of us at the moment, but if you cannot come till October we could be down to eleven!!"

Well, that is one group that I must go to, that is my type of humour.

The distance is about 50 miles away, so I ask her had they got a pub in the village where I could call and get directions. "Yes" she said. "You can call there and the publican will tell you where our hut is.

As sure as night follows day, October came. It was a terrible night, blowing a gale and lashing down with rain, I left a lovely log fire at around 6 o'clock to drive over fifty miles to talk to thirteen dear old ladies (or will it be eleven). I find the pub without any trouble. There is a lovely log fire so I went in and stood by it to get warm. It was still early evening so there were no customers in yet. I turned to look at the fire and on a big oak beam over the fireplace was this amusing verse:–

> We have seen your smiling face,
> We have seen your smart attire,
> But if you are stopping in this place,
> Let's see the bloody fire!!

So I moved, at that moment a small Landlord appeared from somewhere and said to me "You're Alf Strange?"

"Yes I am," I said.

"You are giving a talk to The Evergreens in their hut tonight aren't you?"

"I am indeed," I replied.

"Would you like a drink?" he asked.

"Yes, I will have a scotch and lemonade if I may please".

After he had passed my drink over the bar to me I casually said to him.

"Aren't you having one?"

"Yes, I'll have half a mild" then he added "That will be £1.95p please".

I thought he was buying me one when he asked if I would like a drink, but instead I ended up paying for my drink and his – Ah well, never mind.

"Leave your car on the car park" he told me, "and walk down to the bottom of the car park, turn left and then go about 100 yards then turn left again and you will come to the hut where The Evergreens meet."

I finished my drink and bade him goodnight.

"Call again," he said.

"I will sometime," I answered.

I got my bag of books out of the car, I always take some of my books with me when I give a talk somewhere. It was still pouring with rain when I arrived at the Hut, it was a relic of the 1940-45 war. I imagine it was an ex-army store of some form or other. It was quite small about 20ft by 50ft, as I opened the door a gust of wind nearly blew it off its hinges. I closed it quickly behind me and the thing that struck me was how warm and cosy the room was. It had a large army type stove and around it sat about a dozen or so ladies, all getting on a bit as the old country saying goes. One of them, 80 years old, if she was a day, came down the room to greet me saying

"Are you Mr. Strange?"

The only fellow in the room and she asks me the obvious question, "Are you Mr. Strange".

So for a joke, I said, "No, I am the local Doctor on call and I have received a phone call to say there is a rushed maternity case in this room tonight."

She hesitated for a second then looking me straight in the eye (I will never forget her words)

"It is none of us, we are all on the pill."

Somehow or other a sense of humour has gone out of our society.

We sat around the stove, I told them a few stories, they told me their stories most of which would never pass any censor.

We all reminisced for about an hour, then after a cup of coffee and a piece of cake I wished them all goodnight and headed for home.

Vera as usual was waiting up for me, "How have you got on tonight?" she asked. I had been moaning earlier about having to leave the roaring log fire, turning out on such a wet night and driving 50 miles to talk to about thirteen old ladies.

"Well," I said, "You will not believe me, but it is probably one of the best nights I have ever had."

As I sit here writing on a cold winter's day memories of those types of evenings come flooding back to me, and I often wonder how many of those Senior Citizens that I have talked to over the years still survive today, and what a pity that a lot of them did not write down their memories of their childhood days for future generations. A lot of stories are lost forever with their passing.

A Voice from the Past

One morning I received a letter which read:–

Dear Alf Strange,
   If your Dad's name was Joe who worked at Acton Burnell
in 1905 answer this letter, if he wasn't dunna bother
                                             Signed A. D. Davies.

Well, it was me Dad, Joe Strange and he had worked at
Acton Burnell in 1905 for a blacksmith by the name of Higgs.

So I answered his letter and a week later received another
letter from him, this time telling me all about his early days
in and around Acton Burnell and the Village Smithy. He also
gave his telephone number enabling me to give him a ring
one night, I told him I would like to pay him a visit in the
near future.

"Now, let me see" he said "Meals-on-wheels comes
Mondays, Wednesdays, and Fridays, the Doctor calls most
Tuesdays, the Nurse calls on Thursdays, but it dunna matter
a bugger if they are here, you come when it suits you."

"Thanks, I will," I said and I was just about to put the
phone down when he said: "But dunna you come after a
quarter past nine at night."

"Good Gracious no," I said "I wouldn't dream of coming
at that time of night."

"Well," he said "I always watch the 9 o'clock news and
then I go to the pub for a couple of pints and a game of
dominoes" What a man – ninety two and still able to go to
the pub for a pint and a game of dominoes.

I did eventually go to see him one Saturday morning and
spent a couple of very enjoyable hours in his company, but
sadly he wouldn't talk into my tape recorder. What a pity so
much to tell! However, one story I remember was when his

daughter-in-law and son with whom he lived said: "You tell Alf what happens when you come in from the pub."

"Well," he said, "I always have a bowl of bread and milk."

"Go on" she said, "Well, you have to have a drop of scotch in it" he said. The name of his pub: The Tankerville Arms at Longdon.

A Pikel's Tale

A remarkable coincidence is the story of the pikel which me Dad made for a smallholder by the name of Mr Davies of Hindford. It was a blacksmith-made pikel with a wooden stale. Now this Mr Davies adopted a lad whose name was Jim, a bit older than me and who lived all his life in Hindford.

Eventually he retired and moved to a bungalow in nearby Whittington. Jim Roberts was a typical lad and his main hobby was Whittington Cricket Club. He tended it as one would tend their favourite garden or lawn at home.

But back to the pikel – when Jim retired to his bungalow he gave his pikel, now minus its stale and also a very old scythe to Edward Goff his neighbour and asked him to bring them to me for my Blacksmith Museum. He knew I would treasure them.

After about a year I finally got round to putting a new stale in the pikel, more than 80 years after me Dad had made it for Jim's Dad.

Believe me or believe me not, I had just finished putting in the new stale and was wondering where to hang it on my museum wall, when into my smithy walked a fellow from Whittington. We got chatting and then his words really stunned me, he had called to tell me that Jim Roberts had just passed away in Boots the Chemist in Oswestry. Coincidence!!

21

Dates I will always remember

There are certain dates in ones life that one will always remember.

October 23rd 1980 is one that I will never forget. At 5 a.m. I was awakened by a pain in my chest the like of which I had never had before, I was sweating profusely and I realised immediately that I was in fact having a heart attack. It was like as if my chest was in the grip of a blacksmith's vice.

Vera rang for the Doctor who was with me in a matter of minutes as luckily for me he lives in our village. He gave me a strong injection of morphine to dull the pain and then the system swung into action and within the hour I was in the Coronary Care Unit at the Royal Shrewsbury Hospital. At no time did I lose consciousness and I was full aware of what was happening.

Apparently I was not responding to the various drugs that were being injected into my system. I could sense the concern of the Doctors. One thing I do recall was the age of the Doctors and the thought crossed my mind that I wished they were older, they seemed so young looking. Obviously, they were fully qualified for any situation that arose.

After a brief consultation at the bottom of my bed one of the Doctors came to me and said: "Mr Strange, we are going to give you the electric shock treatment, we will give you a whiff of something to temporary put you out for a few seconds."

The electric shock treatment is to re-start the heart after it had stopped. My heart had not stopped but apparently was not going to go on at the pace it was going for much longer. I do not remember anything of the electric shock but I do recall how the tension eased around my bed and my heart was going at a more acceptable speed. All this had happened before 10 o'clock in the morning. I do remember how sore my ribs felt for a few days. I went on quite well for nearly 48 hours and then the nurse came to me and enquired if I was feeling all right.

Apparently my heart was beginning to fail. Then the Doctor arrived and in no time at all I was in the theatre having an emergency pacemaker fitted at 5 o'clock in the morning.

Again I was fully conscious and knew everything that was taking place. I remember the Doctor saying that my chest muscles were too tough to get the life saving instrument into my heart and he would have to go a more direct way which I believe was a more serious operation.

Next morning at the same time the same procedure. It was something to do with the muscles in my heart that had been damaged from my heart attack. Sister Penny explained to me the technical details of the operation, it was in fact a pacing wire attached to the pacemaker.

I was in intensive care for nearly a week. Sadly, quite a few that came in after me did not make it through the right door, very upsetting for the doctors and nurses to lose a patient. Somehow they always seem to have the time to make a drink for any patient who has just witnessed the death of someone.

Now it's time for me to come out of intensive care and into the main ward, still under strict supervision. Sister Mary Edwards was the sister at the time. She came to me one morning and said " Good news for you Alf, it's the main ward for you tomorrow." I thanked her very much for all she and all her nurses had done for me. Then she said:

"Who is coming to see you this afternoon?"

"Vera will be coming," I replied,

"Yes," she said, "But who will be bringing her?"

"My best pal, Ron," I said.

"Would you like to see him?" she enquired.

"Very much so," was my reply.

"All right," she said, " I will ring Vera and tell her to bring Ron in to see you."

The rule in intensive care is that only close members of

your family are allowed to see you, but as I was on the mend the rule was bent slightly. Ron and Vera came into the ward and were both sitting on the same side of my bed as I was still wired up to the emergency pacemaker.

After about 5 minutes of conversation with Ron and Vera the door opened and in walked a Congregational Minister to see me. Men of the cloth are allowed to visit at any time. He pulled up a chair and sat on the opposite side of the bed to Ron, my mate. After a few moments I realised that on one side of the bed was the parson, and Ron, who was also the local undertaker, was sat on the other, so I claim to be the only person to come out of Intensive Care with the parson on one side of the bed and the undertaker on the other!!

On my travels I occasionally meet that Minister and he always says that he has told that story many times and said what a wonderful sense of humour I had. It was not funny at the time, mind you, but when I look back at that period of my life little did I think then the change it was going to bring for me.

When one goes in to Ward 24, that is another step towards going home. When I came in to Ward 24 I received a little cheer from the other patients, John Tench from Gobowen was one of them. He was working for A.D.A.S. at the time. Another was Bill Fry from Madeley who had been a miner down in South Wales at one time. I remember to this day how he spoke to me, "Alf, I am glad you have made it, if I had known you were coming out today I would have had you in the team for Saturday, but I have only got you down for sub!"

The furthest thought in my head was to think of playing a game of football at that time but such is the sense of humour of our age group.

Bill Fry was a noted wine maker and one night after the day staff had gone off duty they were going to have a party, so Bill said he was going to get his wife to bring in a couple of bottles of nettle wine for them. This she did, and Bill gave them the wine. Next morning the two nurses in question came in to the ward and told Bill what marvellous wine it was and how everyone had enjoyed it.

"How do you make it Bill" they enquired,

"Well" he said "You select some nice big nettles, put them in a big bowl, add bits of this and bits of that then some boiling water and then you wait until it starts to ferment, then I get my dog to go down the field and I watch him very carefully to see which bunch of nettles he cocks his leg on."

"I then pick those nettles and carry them up to the house and shake them on to the fermenting wine in the bowl and that gives them a nice taste and a bit of body."

I will leave you to imagine the look on the nurses, faces, that said it all and I don't think they had any more of Bill's wine.

My first visit to Coronary Care was in 1980 and I was telling the nurses that I had started to write a book about my village of Welsh Frankton and all its characters. I used to tell them the odd story when they had time to listen. Strange's five minutes it was called and to those who have read my books these are stories of yesteryear. Some are stories involving the outside toilet which was usually located as far down the garden path as possible. Some of my stories also tell of my mother's cure for all ills, a spoonful of castor oil. One night one of the nurses said that she had used an outside toilet. I told her that she didn't look old enough to know about them. "Oh yes, I am" came the reply. " I was staying with my uncle on his farm miles from Shrewsbury. His house had not been modernised so his outside toilet was as you say about 30 yards down the garden path. One dark night I wanted to go to the toilet so he lit his old hurricane lamp with a cracked glass, it was a windy night and half way down the garden path a gust of wind blew the lamp out, I was really scared and ran all the way back up to the house."

The other nurse who was standing at the foot of my bed said: "You wouldn't have run back if you had had a spoonful of his mother's castor oil."

I had not had a shave for about a week, well not a decent one anyway. One of the nurses had shaved me with a battery shaver which to say the least could have done with a good sharpening. It would have been better off left alone, my face looked like the back end of a sheep that had been through many thorny hedges.

However I was allowed on my first morning out of intensive care to go in a wheelchair to the toilet and washroom to wash myself still coupled up to my battery and emergency pacemaker.

We don't appreciate being able to do normal everyday things that are taken for granted. A knocking on the toilet door startled me for a moment and I heard a nurse say "Mr Strange, don't on any account use an electric razor, as it will upset your pacemaker." Luckily for me I had used an ordinary safety razor. Coming back in to the ward how good it felt, a good wash and shave and a clean pair of pyjamas.

In the next bed to me was a very overweight gentleman, well I say next bed but he was allowed to sleep in a reclining chair, he was more comfortable like that so he was not requiring to use his bed. He was on a very strict weight reducing diet and had been for some time, but staff could not understand why he was not losing any weight. Apparently his daughter was bringing in some food every night which he was hiding under the sheets on his bed. I used to hear the rustling of paper in the night but I didn't loose him down. One day the nurses decided to change his bed. Crumbs were discovered and all hell was let loose. The nurses gave him a right dressing down, and I can hear him now saying; "But it was only puff pastry." But it was the end of midnight feasts for him.

His daughter came in that night with her usual carrier bag of goodies but got no further than the door. I often wonder how he got on.

Sister Edwards was a delightful nurse who liked a bit of fun. I remember one evening she had come in to the ward with her window prop. It was November and some wanted the windows open and some wanted them left closed, it was a job to please everyone. I found out that she played golf at Sandiway near Chester where Tommy Gardner was the professional. Little did I think I would ever play golf again but such is life. I have had many years of playing and am still doing so nearly twenty years on. I have had many games of golf with Tommy Gardner who can still beat his age on the golf course. Tommy is now over eighty years old and still enjoying his game of golf.

Sadly Sister Edwards died several years ago as did Ron Jones the undertaker from Welsh Frankton, and I was the one who was supposed to go first.

I vowed that when I came home from hospital that if I was lucky enough to get my book published I would donate all my royalties to the Coronary Care Unit and Ward 24. This I managed to do but not without a lot of setbacks. Little did I think I would now be writing my fourth volume about life and country characters in and around my beloved village of Welsh Frankton where I was born some seventy odd years ago, and have only moved house once – a hundred yards in seventy years.

An aged gentleman in the opposite bed to me had recovered from a heart attack and it came time for him to go home. He was in the day room on his own crying. I asked him what was the matter. He said to me: "I don't want to go home, my wife has passed away, I live on my own, and in hospital I have made friends and had good company." I thought to myself: "How sad, nothing to go home for."

When I first came home having been some fifteen days with doctors and nurses never far away, the first night going to bed was quite traumatic. On my own, a phone call away from your doctor, no bell to push by the side of you bed. However as the nights and days passed my confidence began to return, and after about a week or so was able to walk the fifty or so yards to the Dutch barn pillar and back.

Every day a little further for the next six weeks, then back to the Royal Shrewsbury for my first check up.

Ron Hodnett took me in his car. I had a lot of tests and a good report from the doctor whose name I can't remember but he played rugby for Market Drayton, but I remember him saying to me: "Alf, if you look after yourself you could well go on for another five, ten, or fifteen years," I thought "God, I will be seventy by then."

Alas the fifteen years have gone, how I wished he had kept on saying twenty or twenty-five years. However I never dreamed I would have another fifteen years.

Ron and I called at the Fox and Hounds at West Felton for a celebration drink, it being about a week before the Christmas of 1980. Little did I think then that Ike who kept the pub and Ron would pass away before me.

A story I recall at the time was about alcohol, was it good or bad for heart complaints? A doctor was asked that question and he replied that his grandfather had a heart attack and his doctor had said that he could have one glass of scotch a day, but his grandfather had a very big glass! – I leave you to come to your own conclusion on the subject. (I have) and I also have got a very big glass!

Exercise every day was a must and after six months I was able to walk four or five miles a day. On wet days an exercise bike in my shed was the next best thing. Life had taken on a new meaning, time to walk, time to talk, time to listen, time to notice the changing seasons. Snowdrops followed by daffodils, daffodils followed by bluebells and then the fern takes over the woods, and then that dies off in November, everywhere looks so dead. Then in January the snowdrops begin to peep through and the whole cycle begins again – nature has a way of looking after its own.

After about six to nine months of doing no physical work, my own doctor suggested that it was time to try, not many easy jobs in a blacksmith and farmer's set up but as I was receiving the grand sum of £27 per week, this being my sick pay – after six months it was called invalidity benefit. I being self employed and Vera a partner I was not able to claim for her, this after putting stamps on my card for some forty odd years, it was not much to live on. However the time had now arrived for me to do what I had always vowed to do – reconstruct a Village Smithy in a building at Brow Farm, having knocked down the 300 year old Smithy of my Dad's and Grandad's day. Little did I think of all the problems that was going to cause with the system.

I also cleaned out the old railway container that had been

Frankton Cricket Club's first pavilion so that I could use it to do my writing of my book "Me Dad's the Village Blacksmith." As promised all the money raised went to the Coronary Care Unit and Ward 24 at the Royal Shrewsbury Hospital.

Pressure was being put on me by the system. I had now been on invalidity benefit for twelve months. One day a gentleman from Social Security called to see me.

"Mr Strange" he enquired,

"That's me" I replied.

"I see you have constructed a Blacksmith's Shop and I believe you are writing a book" he said,

How he knew I didn't know.

"Yes" I replied "I am."

"Well," he said "we class that as work so you will be signed off as fit for work."

"You don't call writing a book, and constructing a Village Smithy work, I have only used my expertise and have done no lifting" I said.

"Some people class writing a book as work" he replied. I laughed, I thought he was joking, but he wasn't.

A medical at the clinic the following week passed me fit for light sedentary work – the end of my princely sum of £27 per week. However, he said "We can supply you with the equipment to help you farm, to save you having to lift anything, bales of hay, fertiliser, cattle corn etc."

Out the following week came the expert regarding the equipment the system would supply to get me off Invalidity Benefit which was costing the government £1350 a year. The system was going to supply me with a tractor and a hydraulic lift on the back costing in the region of £4000, a conveyor belt to get bales to all around my buildings to save me lifting them. I could roll them into the cattle feeding troughs costing again another £3000. Also another hydraulic lift to lift anything else that was too heavy costing again another £1000 – the total cost to get me back to work, around £8000.

"Thank-you very much" I said "But there is one thing you have forgot, you must remember I am also a farrier about half of my income comes from shoeing horses." There was a silence for a moment

"Right" he said "I will bring out Mr so and so next week, he has worked with horses abroad."

The day arrived, so did Mr so and so with his secretary, this time he had designed a sort of what we call a cattle crush with a hoist on it. Apparently a piece of rope was to be attached to the horse's leg, threaded through a ring and then attached to a ratchet so you could work the ratchet up and down and lift the horses foot up to a reasonable height to save lifting. What the average horse would have thought of it I just don't know.

I was having a job to stop myself from laughing out loud, but he was serious.

"Well" I said "For a start you would have a hell of a job to get a horse into a cattle crush," and I also remarked if his ears touched any part of the crush that would be it, no way will a horse go in to a low building. His next remark really did make me laugh out loud.

"When I was abroad," he said, "The farrier used to knock the horse on the back of the head and when he went down on the ground someone else sat on his head, no need to lift his feet."

My remark to him was that I would like to knock a few of my customers on the head with a hammer but not a horse.

He eventually left leaving me to decide whether to go ahead with his wonderful scheme. The spending of thousands of pounds to get one poor soul back to work. I will never know if his inventions would have worked as I was signed off the following week.

The Ellesmere Exhibition of 1982

Little did I think of the consequences when Felicity Barnett from the village of Lee, my Granny's old village, rang me.

"Alf" she said, "We are running an Ellesmere Exhibition and the committee would like you to open up your old re-constructed Smithy to the public for 3 or 4 days so that people can come and see how blacksmiths worked 100 years ago."

I agreed to open for that once. A bus was run from Ellesmere each morning and afternoon for four days and on one bus load there was about a dozen punks and rockers. I wonder what the older village people would have made of them, punks and rockers watching a village blacksmith at work.!! They were no problem at all and in fact they asked a lot of sensible questions.

I think at a rough guess we had about a thousand people pass through our Smithy on those four days. That is what really started me off doing Blacksmith Demonstrations to the local W.I. and various country groups, and with the publishing of my first book 'Me Dad's the Village Blacksmith' a different life was beginning to take off.

Instead of shoeing horses people seemed to want to hear my stories of the life of not only myself, but also my Granny and Grandad and other people's Grannies and Grandads. Seats had to be provided for different organisations, many small groups of W.I. Mothers Union, Young Wives, Young Farmers, school parties, etc. Coaches instead of horse boxes, cars instead of Landrovers and trailers, – then the system struck again.

Arriving on my yard one morning was a young man from the council.

"Mr Strange?" he asked.

"It is," I replied.

"Have you had planning permission for change of use of this building?."

"No" I replied "I was not aware of that."

Reading some literature and telling me in no uncertain terms that I was breaking the law and there was a possibility that I could be fined £1000 and £100 for every day that I remained open.

"All I am doing different is people are coming to see me in a coach instead of a cattle wagon," I replied.

"Surely" I asked "You are not suggesting that the W.I. can come to see me in a cattle wagon but not a coach."

His reply really shook me.

"Yes" he said "I am."

"Will you put that down in writing?" I asked.

He had no answer to that. When you have survived a heart attack remarks like that don't bother you.

"You will hear more about this," he said, as he drove off in his motor car, possibly getting a petrol allowance as well.

About a fortnight later another young man arrived with what looked like a bigger brief case, but during that fortnight I had done a little bit of research, and had got the support of the W.I. and a chat with the police to see how long they would take to come out and move the ladies of the W.I., who had made plans to temporally block the main road, each carrying a placard saying – "KEEP ALF OPEN."

It would take about half an hour to get them moved. I decided to play my ace card to this young man with his big briefcase.

"I don't know who sent you here this morning, but who ever it was you can go back and tell them that Alf is keeping open and that he has the support of the Women's Institute." And I walked away.

He drove out of my yard and I had no more trouble with that particular department. W.I.'s are no longer just 'Jam and Jerusalem'. They have been known to sway governments. So I suggest to anyone with what they think is a common sense problem to get the W.I. on your side. My one regret is that I never had the chance to film a group of W.I. ladies coming down the tailboard of a trailer pulled by a Landrover. What a picture that would have been. It could have easily made the front pages instead of Charles and Camilla.!!

But that was only one hurdle, there were plenty more to come in the shape of Highways Officialdom.

The main road that runs past Brow Farm has quite a steep hill hence the name 'The Brow.' I have had battles with all departments since 1965.

I say 'The Brow' is dangerous, the police say 'The Brow' is dangerous, so do Ellesmere Road Safety Committee and 90% of the people who live in the area say it is dangerous, yet nothing is done about it.

I asked one certain highway official how many people have to be killed before you do anything, and his reply shocked me. "About eight," he said.

I reacted to that immediately by saying: "Well, as long as it's not your wife and family that would be all right." He just walked away without a word.

In 1963 plans were made to take the hump off the top of The Brow at a cost of about £25,000 but as with a lot of other schemes there was no money in the Council Budget that year for it to be done. Now some thirty odd years later the cost would be more like £250,000. One of the reasons given for that figure is that the, e.g., water, electricity and telephones would have to be moved into the field and apparently it would cost about £50,000 to move each service.

In 1960 the mains water pipe had not gone through and the electricity and telephone services were on poles overhead, lack of thought by the powers that be. Why on earth the three services were not put inside the field which meant they would not have to be moved now thus saving approx. £150,000, but a village blacksmith must not make remarks like that as to the short sightedness of the powers that be in putting the services under the road instead of in the field, lack of commonsense.

The Moment of Truth

Having done a lot of walking and also riding my exercise bike, I received a telephone call from Carl at Llangollen who was in charge of the horse drawn boats on the canal. His blacksmith had called it a day and wanted to pack up working, I believe he was well in to his seventies. Carl's request was that I should go and shoe his three horses, Duke, Spot and Fred.

"These three horses will be very quiet to shoe," he said, but no matter how quiet they are, a fair bit of physical strength is still required to shoe a horse, especially ones the size of those three. With a chat to my Doctor who asked "Have you got to shoe a horse to provide you with income?."

The answer to that was "No."

"Well" he said "If you have not got to shoe a horse, then don't. Be it on your own head, but if you do decide to shoe a horse again and feel any pain or discomfort, stop immediately and sit down."

I had not told him that I had already made a set of shoes for Duke!

Saturday morning was the day chosen to shoe my first horse in over two years. Feeling a bit apprehensive, I arrived at Llangollen. The wharf side along the Shropshire Union Canal is where the horses are stabled. Duke was tied up to the railings waiting patiently to be shod. I have a feeling that he knew that I was a bit concerned as to how I was going to feel because he literally picked up his near fore foot for me. At this stage again I must say that from a financial point of view I had no need to shoe a horse again. I got the two front feet ready to put shoes on.

After fitting the shoes hot, I cooled them down in the nearby canal, then I nailed the shoes on and my brother Jack clenched them up. I felt O.K. then the same procedure with the back two feet and Duke was shod. We put a spot of oil on his hooves and Duke looked quite smart. I can not explain how I felt, a really great feeling crept over me, to be able to do it again, what one had been bought up to do – Shoe a Horse.!

As always when shoeing horses at Llangollen wharf quite a crowd of people usually gathered to watch us shoe a horse. I have known as many as forty or more people gather to watch us shoe a horse, and this morning was no different. I can remember it was the Saturday before the Easter holidays, sitting down on my shoeing box having a drink of Carl's coffee, Carl asked me if I would be able to shoe Fred and Spot some time in the near future. This was arranged but only one at a time. I did not want to chance providence too much and as with a lot of my stories there is a sequel.

A young man came up to me with his wife and children obviously on holiday in Llangollen, he remarked to me: "I have been watching you shoeing that horse, you really do know your job."

I replied: "Well, I have been shoeing horses for over forty years."

Then he said to me: "I am a farrier."

"Where are you from?" I enquired, and at the same time thinking to myself what was he doing here on a Saturday morning, he should be shoeing horses at home!

"Oh!" he said, "I don't shoe horses any more. It is hard work and there is no money in it. Look at you at your age having to work on a Saturday morning."

I didn't tell him any different, but as said before, it is one of life's pleasures to be able to work. For many more years I shod the horses at Llangollen and I have met many people from all parts of the world, some of them in the shop there where many of my books have been sold.

The Diva and The Anvil Chorus

Jack an I arrived one weekend at Llangollen Wharf to shoe one of the barge horses, there were crowds of people there, television cameras everywhere, the world's press and dignitaries of all shapes and sizes. I thought at last fame must have arrived for me, but alas, no, it was not to be. A famous soprano of Russian origin was to be interviewed, as she had won a competition the night before. She was going to sing sitting on one of the boats. Jack and I started to get ready to shoe the horse but the world's press treated us with contemptuous looks – two blokes in working class clothes. Jack began to take the shoes off Fred just as this world renowned singer with her entourage burst into song accompanied by the tap, tap, tap of hammer on iron. Then a voice shouted "STOP, STOP!" Headphones were being adjusted as the sound from the anvil and hammer were interfering with the recording. A man came up to me and in broken English said: "Vat are you doing? You are ruining my broadcast."

"No one said anything to me," was my reply, "I have come to shoe this horse."

"You vil have to stop," he said.

"No, you wait until we have finished," I said.

The Berlin Wall had just been taken down, but at that particular time I think Russian and British relations were at an all-time low!

Then he said: "Please vil you vait for 10 minutes or so and we will be able to do our recording?" We agreed to do just that, and the cold war was off again. I often smile at that particular incident and wonder what if we had not stopped our shoeing. The Tower of London maybe or a Siberian saltmine. Just another incident on the life of a village blacksmith.

Lamb Chops for Luck

Little did I think when I rang a telephone number what an eventful day that would be. An advert appeared in the Shropshire Star one evening – 'For Sale a mini pickup'.

At the time I was looking for a better pickup as my own pickup was requiring a lot of repairs. An appointment was made with the lady owner of the said vehicle. She was very Welsh.

Arriving at the farm the mini pickup was out on the yard, it had been washed and polished, it was quite a tidy looking vehicle, and it would be o.k. for my job. Then the lady appeared and started to tell me all the good points about her pickup – no bad ones!

Then the all-important question arose – the price. She was adamant she would not take a penny less than £650. I thought for a moment then offered her £590, £60 less than she wanted. I had been bought up to always start your bidding low. Me Dad used to say: 'You can always go up with your offer but not come down.'

Waiting for a moment or two for her reply, I'd guessed she wanted to sell her pickup, her reply was: "I will not take any less than £640."

"Look" I said "You want to sell the pickup, I want to buy it, my final offer to you is £600, take it or leave it, I have got to go and look at another one."

Turning to walk towards my car to leave, she came after me and said "Look if you will give me £610 for it I will give you two lamb chops for your tea."

"You can give me two lamb chops" I said "but I am still only willing to give you £600 for your pickup."

"O.K." she said, and the deal was made.

The mini pickup has served me well for many years, a fair price all round.

I often have a little smile when I think of the offer of two lamb chops for my tea.

Just another little story in the life of a village blacksmith!!

The oldest visitor to the museum. 100 years difference in age. Grandaughter Emily 1, and Mrs. Kathleen Beard, 101 years.

A Sad Day at Llangollen

Old Duke had been failing in health for some time and an X-ray had found cancer of the stomach and it was kinder to put him down than let him suffer. I went up to take his shoes off for the last time. He was however not sent for dog meat. A grave was dug in his field by a digger and Old Duke was buried in his field overlooking the canal.

He had pulled the boats up and down for many years. I kept one of his shoes as a keepsake, so ends the story of Duke, a faithful old friend.

He was the first horse I had shod again after my own illness. I shall remember him for the rest of my days.

Rest in Peace, Duke – 'The King of the Cut.'

Duke pulling the boat full of people along the canal at Llangollen.

39

Outside Loo

Many different names over the years have been produced, some of which I would not get passed the censor, but I am going to tell some true stories about that building 6ft by 4ft normally built of bricks and mortar with a galvanised roof. The only lighting in it would be about two bricks left out of one of the walls, no electric light in my early childhood, so the hurricane lamp or a lighted candle was a very important household facility. And what was a toilet roll? The daily paper was a must, and if you had time it was surprising what little stories one had missed.

My first story about the outside toilet was one afternoon not many years ago I was speaking at a Ladies Conservative meeting in a Midlands town. 150 Conservative Ladies and Alf Strange, the Village Blacksmith taking the place of a Bishop. Out of those 150 Ladies only 3 of them knew I was the village blacksmith. The other 147 thought they were going to listen to an address by the Bishop who was indisposed and I had stepped in at short notice to speak at their dinner, and my theory in life is "Be what you are, dunna try to be what you inner."

After my talk, I was handed the Visitors Book to sign my name in. One of the names before me was Sir Winston Churchill who had signed his name and occupation as Member of Parliament, so I signed my name Alf Strange - Village Blacksmith!

My talk went down very well, and I was about to leave for home, one lady came to me and said: "Thank you, Alf, for your talk and your stories about the outside toilet, one of which took me back to 1939." She said: "It was October of that year, my husband and I had been married in the September and he was immediately called up to the Royal Air

Force." Now the majority of my readers know what happened in September 1939, it was the month the 1939-45 war began with Hitler's Germany. Telling me this story, she went on: "You must remember I was a town girl and not used to country ways and had always been used to a flush toilet and a bathroom in the house, not a toilet 50 yards or so from the house."

"My husband was posted to an air base in a country district miles from anywhere, but luckily for us he had managed to persuade the squire of the village to let him have the use of a country cottage in the middle of a big wood and I was able to move in there with him.

"Imagine the shock to me, a 'townie' to find that the toilet was about another 50 yards or so down the wood, but we were both so happy to be together as thousands of other couples were parted. The problem with the toilet was there was no door on it, it had never had a door on it, no need for one in the middle of a big thick wood. I was using the toilet one morning, the sun was shining, it was a really lovely October morning, when all of a sudden a fox ran past the toilet door. I was scared to death, not knowing what to do, and being a 'townie' not used to country ways so I thought I would sit where I was. A few minutes later a pack of hounds went racing past, now I was in a state sitting there and trembling. After what seemed like hours up rode a man wearing a red coat, riding a large grey horse. He must have been a perfect gentleman because he raised his hat to me and said "Good Morning, Madam, which way did they go?"

Another time I was speaking to a group of senior citizens at Shrewsbury. I know Shrewsbury reasonably well, The Morris Hall, The Music Hall, a Hall at Monkmoor, The Shirehall and many others. But this one afternoon I was not too familiar with the hall I was speaking at, so I decided to go a little earlier park my car and walk to this place. Instead of being early I was late getting to Shrewsbury. Standing on a street corner, I spotted a dear old lady making haste along the opposite pavement, I thought: "I bet she is going to this particular hall," so I crossed over the street to her.

"Excuse me," I said, "Are you going to a Senior Citizens meeting in the hall?"

"Yes" was her quick reply.

"Do you mind if I come with you?" I enquired,
Not pausing in her step, she answered;

"You inner o'wd enough."

"Well" I said "I am still coming with you."
Little did I realise what a wonderful story she had to tell. Eventually some time later she came to Brow Farm with her son to see me and she told me this wonderful story.

When she was first married in 1937, she and her husband lived in Madeley near Wellington and they used to cycle from Madeley to Llandudno for their weeks summer holiday. They used to break their journey half way and stay the night with an old aunt who was a little eccentric. Her hobby was collecting Christian signs and mottos, she had dozens of them hanging all around the house, such as 'Jesus Loves Me' 'Christ is Risen' and 'Trust in the Lord'. She went on to tell me she even had some hanging in the outside toilet. The one she remembers best was the one hanging over the door as you were sitting on the toilet looking at it, 'Mine eyes are always on thee, sayeth the Lord.'

Speaking at St Martins' Methodist Chapel one Tuesday afternoon having just given my usual talk, one dear old lady got up and said that when she was young her Granny had come to stay with them for a few weeks, and every night at around 9 o'clock, she had to light the hurricane lamp and accompany her Granny to the outside toilet, and six nights out of seven all she had was a touch of wind!!

I like this story told to me by a farmer. The farmer's wife said to her husband one morning; "Let's pack up; we have been farming now for nigh on 50 years, I have had enough so let's retire." The farmer thought for a moment or two and then said:

"We will go on for a bit longer, you never know what money we will need."

"Right," said the farmer's wife, "If we have got to go on I insist we have an inside toilet."

Her husband said: "Have you gone mad woman, don't you realise the cost?"

"Sell one of your little fields, that will be enough for an inside toilet," she said.

This her husband did.

His wife said "I am going to the builders today to see when he can start."

"Owd your hand a bit" said her husband. " I am going to invest the money from the field and when the interest is enough, we will use that for the inside toilet." Many more years went by and eventually the farmer's wife got her inside toilet.

"Right" she said "Now, I want a nice new outside brick built barbecue, now that I have got a nice new toilet, I am going to do a bit of entertaining, and I want to do it in the next few months, I am not waiting until we have enough interest from the field money".

Six months later she had her new outside barbecue. To save some of the expense her husband had been helping the builder, mixing the cement and carrying the bricks for the barbecue etc. He had not seen one of his mates for many months, bumping into him one night, his mate said "Where on earth have you been?" "Oh" the husband said "My missus is spending money like water, and all I can see is – we are doing inside what we used to do outside, and we are doing outside what we used to do inside!!"

Smithy and Farm Museum

By now we were averaging a coachload of people a day, aged from 5 years old to 95 years old which prompted me to write this fourth book, I knew that I would have enough material

One day we had a party from a home in St Martins, a village about 5 miles away, a very aged party, some in wheelchairs, some able to walk with the aid of a walking frame.

Three 'stories' happened that day. One 89 year old lady wanted to use the toilet and because the gents happened to be vacant I suggested she popped in there to save her walking up the yard to use the ladies toilet. She was in the toilet for several minutes and when she came out I jokingly said " What have you been doing in there?" She answered me straight away "I have been writing on the walls!" 89 years old and still with a sense of humour.

She was also very Welsh and of course I asked her what part of Scotland she came from?! The answer I got in no uncertain terms was Llanfyllin, Boyo!

We have three ladies toilets, one on its own, the original one, which has been modernised, but the other two new ones are about 50 yards further up the yard. I always tell the coach parties this before they get off the coach.

One day about 25 dear old ladies were queuing at the first toilet and my wife Vera went to them to say "You are aware there are two more toilets further up the yard."

"We are all together," was their reply.

Another day, an aged gentleman dashed off the bus and straight into the gents toilet and bolted the door in a hurry so no one else could get in. He was in there rather a long time so I mentioned to one of the 'helpers' that there was an old lad that had been in there for a quite a while. On that, the door opened and out came the old gent. His mate who had been waiting to go in to the toilet said " I thought when you had that curry yesterday you would be in trouble – so keep off the curry today."

The Vicar's Farewell

One of my favourite stories concerns The Village Blacksmith and the Vicar.

Many years ago well before the 1939-45 war, there were not many motor cars on the road. The vicar called one day to see the blacksmith and on his smithy yard was a motor car. The vicar asked the blacksmith whom the motor car belonged to, to which the blacksmith replied: "It is mine."

This rather took the vicar by surprise.

"How on earth can you afford to buy a motor car in times like these" he enquired.

"I can't," said the blacksmith.

"The reason I own that car is that one of my old aunts has passed away, and left me her car in her will."

"Well inna you lucky" said the vicar.

"Well, I suppose I am" replied the blacksmith, "but I am too old to learn to drive, so it won't be a lot of good to me."

"I can drive," said the vicar.

"Well, with you only working one day a week," said the blacksmith, "you have plenty of time to learn."

The vicar ignored that remark and said to Bill the blacksmith:

"Lend me your car next Tuesday to go and preach at another church about 5 miles away at a Harvest Festival service please"

"If you lend me your car it will save me biking there, and why don't you come with me?"

"All right" said Bill the blacksmith "I will come with you, but remember I don't know the first things about cars."

"Leave it to me" said the vicar.

Away the two men went, but, alas, about half a mile from the church the car stopped – no petrol!!

The vicar said to Bill the blacksmith "Why didn't you put some petrol in the car?"

The old blacksmith said: "What is petrol?"

The vicar said "It is the stuff that makes the car go."

It was no use arguing.

Away they both went to a farm about 200 yards away. The vicar knocked on the door, a very old farmer answered it.

"I don't suppose you have such a thing as a drop of petrol?"

The farmers answer was the same as the blacksmiths – "What is petrol?"

Now I am sure you have all been to a church or chapel and how often have you heard the preacher talking about having Faith in the Lord – you must have Faith to go through this wicked world.

The old farmer then said "Oh, my son has just bought a new tractor."

"Will there be petrol in that" asked the vicar "can we go and see?"

"Certainly" said the old farmer "help yourself."

Yes, there was petrol in the new tractor, but what on earth could they find to carry it in. Eventually, the only thing they could find to hold the petrol was that wonderful piece of equipment which in those days was kept under the bed – 'The chamber pot'.

The vicar proceeded down the road to the motor car, walking very steady so as not to spill any of the petrol.

He arrived back at the motor car and proceeded to empty the chamber pot in to the petrol tank of the car.

At this stage another farmer and his wife went by in his pony and trap, they were going to the same church as the vicar was preaching.

Turning to his wife he said "There's Faith for you!"

Blacksmith turned Actor

As I sit here writing on a cold wet January morning I wonder if anyone has ever realised out of the hundreds of phone calls one receives over the years, a single call can change one's life dramatically, as did a phone call from Lily Morgan regarding Riding for the Disabled some 21 years ago.

That gave me a different outlook on life. Another call some 13 years ago gave me another insight into a completely different world and class of people from what a humble village blacksmith had ever met. Little did I know what I had let myself in for.!

A voice on the other end of the telephone enquired if I would be able to help them out in shows they were putting on at Erddig Hall near Wrexham.

A group of professional actors were reliving a day in 1910, the day of the coronation of King George V and Queen Mary at Erddig Hall which is owned by The National Trust.

Squire Philip Yorke had given Erddig Hall to the National Trust.

The voice said they had been trying everywhere to find a village blacksmith to work the old village smithy, which had been restored to its former glory. It was for three weeks only, with two shows a day. Six actors from The Young National Trust Theatre Players were to take over the different parts of the staff. Squire Yorke, The Butler, The Estate Carpenter, The Housekeeper, The Kitchen Maid and also one character was to play the part of a Tramp.

Coach loads of children were to arrive from schools everyday to 'Go Back in Time.' Each actor was to have six or seven children with him or her dressed up in period costume of the age i.e. six little squires, six little tramps. Six little

butlers, six little house maids, six little housekeepers and six little carpenters.

The idea was to take children back in time to what life was like yesteryear.

They would come through to the smithy in separate groups to watch me working for about 10 minutes or so and also to ask any questions about my work as a blacksmith. Different groups would ask different questions. I found this very interesting, but I was surprised how little they knew about things of the past.

The value of work had been so different in 1910 – three shillings for shoeing a large horse, (approx. 15p)

In 1982 £35 for the same four shoes, as a matter of interest, today's price in 1999 would be as much as £70 to £80.

Four young girls were looking around the smithy whilst I was busy explaining to some others in the group what the various old tools were for, when I realised my smithy fire needed to be blown up by the old hand operated bellows so I asked the four young girls would they mind blowing my fire up. They obliged by blowing on the smithy fire, – with their mouths!

This made me realise that unless they were shown various things, there would be age groups that may never know what blacksmith bellows were for. This made me more determined than ever to carry on with my own blacksmith demonstrations at home, despite all the 'aggro' I had been through with the system of the North Shropshire District officer, and still a lot more to come.

Every day at Erddig was a really lovely day with all the actors and the children playing their parts.

I was allowed, being one of the 'staff' to wander around where I wanted and I used to take my 'butties' and a flask of coffee with me. What could be nicer than to be sitting on a seat in the garden admiring the beauty of Erddig Hall and all its surroundings as I wait to begin my afternoon demonstrations.

There was no need to change my Victorian cap and

overalls, I could just sit there thinking how lucky I was to be alive, having survived another heart attack a little earlier.

One day, I noticed someone watching me from a distance after I had finished my demonstrations for the day.

Apparently, he was one of the guides keeping an eye on any would be vandals or 'yobbos.' I suppose in my old blacksmith's clothes and a half-grown beard I did look a bit rough. He did apparently report me to Erddig Officials saying "He was wandering around everywhere, and then blow me he got into a B.M.W. and drove away."

The three weeks of acting and demonstrating blacksmithing, taking the part of the Estate Blacksmith of 1910 were fast coming to an end, just two more shows. The young actors and the two producers had arranged an evening get-together at a wine bar in Llangollen. Vera and I were invited to go with them.

Still not fully fit after my heart attack we decided to go in our own car and not in their mini bus. I wanted to get home at a reasonable hour as I still had one more demonstration to do the following morning. As I recall the actors had bought some of their own drinks with them, litre bottles of red wine, called I think 'plonk.' The evening went with a swing, everyone letting their hair down. Vera and I were introduced to food we had never even heard of. We managed to slip away and left them enjoying their plonk for quite some time after.

Arriving at Erddig next morning to get the smithy fire going and be ready for the actors and children to come through the smithy. As the various groups of children were arriving with actors I realised the previous evening was beginning to take its toll, leaving me a little more to do, talking to the children.

All went through until the last party of children came through, it was Cam, with his party of little tramps. During the three weeks I had taught Cam how to strike for me using a 7lb sledge hammer, helping me to make a cart horse shoe. As he came through the smithy door looking a whiteish, greyish, colour I realised it would be better if he left the sledgehammer where it was and I would manage without him. But, no, he insisted, much to my dismay, that he was going to do his share of the work.

After he had missed hitting the anvil a few times, never mind the shoe, he agreed with me and let me carry on on my own. I bade them all farewell later on in the morning.

Before I close this chapter on my life as an actor, I say 'Thank-you' to all of them, wherever they may be, and many times I have thought of them. Their lifestyle was the way to live, not much money, but the ability to enjoy life. I do know that one was a violin player in the London Philamonic Orchestra and was on loan to the National Trust Players his name was Roddy Streeping.

Also some time later the girl who took the part of the housekeeper was seen regularly on BBC TV hosting the children's programme 'Playschool' her name was Sheila Gilby.

I will never forget those three weeks at a time in my own life just after a serious illness.

Alf and a visitor taking raffle tickets out of the pot his mother once used to make rice pudding.

End of an Era

After a few days rest to recharge my batteries and a lot of thinking done, I started to remodel my own village smithy which I had reconstructed. I realised I had to have a better form of seating for the different groups and organisations that would be coming through.

I had arrived home after a session with my accountant talking about my future plans for my smithy and how I was going to expand it and go further afield with my adverts and talks. She did not seem too keen on my scheme and made some remark that she thought I was too old. !! I replied to her "Winston Churchill was not made Prime Minister until he was 65." She then told me not to get too carried away.

That remark made me more determined than ever, and that night, it must have been fate, for I heard there were some chapel pews for sale at a redundant chapel at Maesbury, just the type of seating I was looking for. A meeting was arranged with the Deacon of the chapel. I bought all the chapel pews, which was really more than I required, but Ron, my best mate, said he would take the surplus ones I had to spare.

We arranged to fetch the pews the following Saturday morning. With the help of young Ron and Richard Dutton who brought his tractor and trailer we arrived at Maesbury chapel.

The Deacon met us there and I realised it was the end of an era for him. Tears were in his eyes. The lads Ron and Richard were keen to get on with the job. The pews were nailed to the floor, still in place as were the pulpit and the organ, the same as they had been for many years.

In no time at all one pew after another were unceremonicly wrenched from the floor and loaded on to the trailer, when suddenly strains of music came from the organ.

It was the Deacon's daughter playing the organ for the last time, I believe she was in her sixties.

We all stopped in our tracks, and a silence fell over the chapel, I felt terrible and I thought to myself: "What on earth are you doing Alf ?" Over 100 years of history are destroyed in a matter of a few hours. It was like someone said to me: "If you had not bought the chapel pews someone else would have done so."

As we carried on with the demolition job I noticed that there was one special pew – a two seater and highly polished. I put it to one side as I thought I would take that in my own pick-up so that it would not get scratched, as I had a special place to put it in the hall at Brow Farm.

The remainder of the pews was now loaded and the two lads were keen to get on their way with their load. They left me talking to the Deacon, tears were now streaming down his face and I was close to tears myself. I wonder what my Mother would have said, having bought up a family of 5 lads to be strong Congregationalists, but as they say: 'Life must go on.'

Picking up the nice little two seater pew and putting it in my pick-up, the deacon came to me, tears still in his eyes and said: "I have just realised that I have not kept a pew for my own family to have in memory of their chapel." I will leave you to guess which pew he had and I also delivered it to his daughter's house.

The chapel pews have caused many comments in my smithy by the thousands of people who have sat on them watching Jack and myself working on our demonstrations. Hanging on the wall is the offertory box with a lock on it and hundreds of pounds have been put in it over the years for Ward 24 Coronary Care Unit and the Ellesmere branch of The British Heart Foundation.

Was it fate that the accountant said: "Don't get carried away," and was it fate that at the same time I heard about the chapel pews. I wonder.

The latest plan forming in my head is we may hold weddings over the anvil. One day, the Brow Smithy may be as famous as the Gretna Green Smithy. But before that happens you can well depend on it there will be more aggro from North Shropshire District Council and the Highways Authority. Ah well, we will see, I expect they will be more worried than I.

Absent Friends – 1946-99

Little did one think what would be the sequel to a meeting that took place 50 years ago. Harry Hughes, Postmaster of Oswestry Post Office and Bill Strange a postal officer at the same Post Office whose home village was Welsh Frankton, met to have a quiet Christmas drink in the Old Stone House pub in Church Street, Oswestry. It was on a Wednesday lunch time. Both men had been doing their War Service. Bill in the Middle East for some 5 years, Harry in the Royal Navy.

One drank white rum, the other red. It was the Wednesday before the Wednesday before Christmas Day 1946.

These two shook hands and decided that 12 months to the day they would meet again. Alf Strange, Bill's brother was invited to have a Christmas drink with them. The following year Doug Gough and Jack Strange joined the trio, and a toast was drunk to 'Absent Friends.'

Other friends were invited to join in the celebrations, and it was decided to change the lunchtime drink to an evening one, as the party had grown and one's afternoon work had begun to suffer.!!

After many different pubs had been visited. Always on the Wednesday before the Wednesday before Christmas, then for many years the venue was The Fox and Hounds at West Felton, Dora and Ike's pub. Vera my wife used to make all the refreshments, some for Dora and Ike as well.

50th Anniversary of Absent Friends 1996.

By now the party was something like 20 in number. All good things come to an end and when Ike left the Fox and Hounds another venue had to be found. No longer could you book a room and take your own butties. Eventually we ended up at 'Ye Olde Boote Inn at Whittington some 10 years ago, but always on the Wednesday before the Wednesday before Christmas!!

The party is now something like 30 to 35 in number. Sons have joined their Fathers. A tie was purchased, well 18 ties to be correct. It is navy blue and has a crest on it showing a foaming pint of beer and the initials A.F. – 'Absent Friends. We still have 16 of those ties left and the order of the day is when The Good Lord calls you your tie is handed in to the 'Big Three' to decide who should have it. One of those ties was unfortunately lost in the moving of houses. But the other one was foolishly swapped for some insignificant American type tie. The said member who did that is still a staunch member and he will never be allowed to forget that because every year he is reminded of it.

Harry, one of the founder members has gone to pastures new, and Bill sadly passed away on November 6th 1999. Many others have passed away over the years, but one hopes they will be looking down on us when at the end of the evening the toast will be drunk to 'Absent Friends'. After many years of searching we eventually found the two sons of Harry Hughes, Dave and Peter. They are now staunch members of our little group.

One hopes our group will go on for many years and that soon grandchildren will be old enough to join this non-political, non religious group.

The Reverend and The Mothers' Union

It was a very hot sweltering evening, one of the hottest days of the year, when Rev Tony Villiers the Rural Dean of Llanymynech arrived at my smithy with a party of ladies from the Mothers Union of his church. It was the kind of evening which would have been better spent having an ice-cream by the mere in Ellesmere from Chris Brown's ice-cream parlour or perhaps having a long cold drink at one of the pubs in Ellesmere, but no, they came for a blacksmith's demonstration then they were going on for a meal and a drink at the Narrowboat Inn.

I don't think that Tony was aware of what awaited him. We togged him up in a Victorian style hat and waistcoat and blacksmiths apron, but he still left his dog collar on. I then invited him to blow the bellows for me to make a horseshoe.

After less than 5 minutes he whispered to me that he was too hot and could he take his collar off. This he did. Our demonstration of making a horseshoe, poker etc lasted a good half hour. By this time we both looked as if we had just walked out of a pool. Our faces were red and our clothes were wringing wet. What we would have given for an ice-cream or a cool pint of shandy when suddenly one dear old lady shook everyone by saying to the Rev Tony "I have been watching you blowing the bellows getting the fire nice and hot, and I reckon when you go to pastures new you'll make a damm good stoker" !!

We all roared with laughter. I can add nothing to this story, only to let the reader draw his or her own conclusions. Remarks like those are so typical of country people, spontaneous and unrehearsed. No offence meant and none taken. I believe they had a good time later at the Narrowboat.

Sticky End

On another very hot sweltering July evening a party of W.I. members from Weston Lullingfields came to visit the smithy. They were the first party to sit on the 'Chapel Pews'. Little did they know what fate would befall them before they went to the Narrowboat Inn for their meal. We had recently re-varnished the pews with a dark oak varnish, and we had left them out in the sun to dry. We had no carpet runners to put on the seats for people to sit on.

Comments were made "How nice it was to have such lovely pews to sit on".

My demonstration and talk went down very well, but then came the time for the ladies to leave. Quite a few were stuck fast to their seats. Discreet glances were made as one after the other disentangled their pretty summer dresses, showing more than what a village blacksmith was intended to see!!

Thank goodness they were a country W.I. and could see the funny side of it. No insurance claim. But I sometimes wonder what would have happened if they had been a party of models out for the evening.

No need for my fertile horseshoe!

My demonstration of blacksmithing includes the making of a cart horse shoe, a poker and a little hook which was used to hang an old fashioned kettle over an open fire. These are given to the visiting party for a free raffle. In my talk I explain that whoever wins the horseshoe is guaranteed fertility. I always get some quite remarkable remarks from my audience.

One gentleman of 86 asked if he could have 5 of them!!. A lady who was a mother of six children said that if she won the horseshoe she would keep it under her pillow to hit her husband on the head with. Another remark was from an 80 year old lady who said if it worked for her it would be a miracle as she had never been married, and so the stories went on and on.

One Saturday night a party came to my smithy dressed in Victorian clothes, ladies in lovely long dresses and lovely old fashioned hats. The men were in black suits and bowler hats. They were going to an 'olde tyme' dance in another village. Amongst the party was a very pretty girl of about 22 years old, who won my 'fertility' horseshoe. As she rose from her seat to collect the shoe, one could see that she was about 8 ? months pregnant. This attracted a remark from one of her party –

"My God I have never known a lucky horseshoe to work that quick!!"

After one of my demonstrations an irate lady rang me to say that she had a complaint to make.

"Oh dear," I said " and what is your complaint about?"

"Well," she said "my mother came to see your demonstration and she bought a 'lucky' horseshoe from your wife and the next day, she fell and broke her leg"!!

My reply wasn't appreciated. I said:

"What a good thing she bought a lucky horseshoe, as she may have fallen down and broke both her legs."

Another gentleman arrived one day and said to me he had been to one of my demonstrations with his wife. He went on to say that he really did not want to come as he had had a new freezer delivered that day. He said that he had enjoyed his night out and when they arrived home as it was rather late they decided to leave the freezer in the outside shed. But on getting up the following morning, to his dismay his freezer had been stolen.

I asked him if he had bought a 'lucky' horseshoe ?

"No," he replied

"Well," I said "there you go, if you had bought a lucky horseshoe your freezer may not have been stolen."

After fifty years of working for all sorts you must always have an excuse for one thing or another.

"What are we going to do today?" Alf and brother Jack.

The offer of a job

It was a lovely morning, the sun was shining, Brow Farm was looking its best, and I was taking in the views from our car park and thinking how lucky I was to live in such a lovely part of the world. Leaving the car park I walked across the paddock and I had been leaning on the fence for about five minutes, when I had a feeling someone was watching me. I turned to look back across the car park and leaning against the rails was a large man in shirtsleeves with his arms covered in tattoos and just beyond him was a lorry, he was obviously its driver. In my daydreaming, I had not heard him arrive on the car park.

Lorry drivers are always pulling up to ask the way to various destinations and we are situated on a main road from Whitchurch to Oswestry at the top of a steep hill.

"Hello," I said, "can I help you?"

"Do you live here?" he said.

"Yes," I replied.

He was a really rough looking character and his next comment really surprised me.

"Ain't you bloody lucky," he said.

"I am," I replied "and where do you live?" I enquired.

"In the middle of bloody London," he replied,

"I don't suppose you would swop with me?" he asked.

"No, thanks," I said, "but it does rain and blow and we do have falls of snow."

"Perhaps you do, but the air you breathe is worth a guinea an ounce," he replied.

I then directed him on his way to City Meats of Rednal. He bade me farewell and remarked "I will call again."

He had hardly gone a hundred yards down the road when on to the car park arrived a fish and chip van, but apart from the gas stove everything else had been taken out and an old camp bed had been fitted in.

Out of it emerged a pretty bare-footed girl of about 23 or 24 years old, she was very attractive with dark hair and a slightly oriental coloured skin.

"Alf Strange?" she asked.

"It is" I replied.

"Have my two friends called to see you, with two ponies and a gypsy caravan?"

"No" I answered.

"Oh well, they are calling to see you, they are on their way from up North to Exeter in the South."

"That is a hell of a long way to travel with two ponies," I said

On that she said "I will go and meet them and direct them to your place."

"What do they want to see me about?" I enquired.

"Oh, just for a chat in general," she replied and away she went in the converted fish and chip van.

I thought to myself we get all sorts calling here, one minute a six foot plus burly lorry driver, and a few minutes later a pretty charming girl who would not have disgraced herself if she had entered a Miss World Contest.

Later on in the day the two men arrived with their ponies and a gypsy caravan. They would be about 25 years old with longish hair, and dressed in tatty shirts and shorts. They unharnessed the two ponies and turned them into the paddock to graze and get a drink of water.

"And what story have you got to tell me?" I asked

As soon as they began to speak I could tell that they had not just been educated at a village school, more like Oxford or Cambridge, a very cultured manner.

"What do you both do for a living? I asked, their reply really shook me.

"We are both professional agitators."

I laughed at that remark.

"And what do you agitate?" I asked.

"The falling of trees and the making of new by-passes and also the decimation of the countryside in general."

62

"You can't stop progress," I remarked.

"It's not progress doing what the system is doing," they said.

And do you know after listening to them for about half an hour or so it made me wonder who was right and who was wrong.

"The Professional Agitators"

More roads mean more cars, more pollution and more accidents.

I asked them if the police ever 'roughed' them up.

"Only occasionally" was their reply "perhaps the police had had a bad night."

"Well are you not afraid of getting hurt?" I asked.

The one replied which made me smile.

"Well if you are up the top of a tall tree that the contractors are going to fell and they start up their chainsaw, brother I am soon down."

"What does your friend who called to see me this morning do for a living?" I asked.

63

"Oh she is quite educated," one said "she is a school teacher."

I could have listened to them all day and they really did want me to go with them. As they left I thought to myself who is really right, is the 'system' right in felling trees. If all the trees in the world were felled we would all be starved of oxygen and as I finish this chapter I thought what a cross section of people, I meet all sorts and yet I myself have only moved about 100 yards in 73 years!!.

Fred Gregory

Today is a typical November day, heavy showers and low clouds in the sky.

It is the day of Fred Gregory's funeral in Welsh Frankton Churchyard. As I was sitting in the church waiting for the funeral party to arrive my thoughts went back to the year of 1936. It was the first time I had met Fred who was a blacksmith and a farrier. He had come to work for me Dad in our own village smithy at the Perthy, I would be about 11 years old at the time, (was that really 62 years ago?)

While sitting there my mind kept going back to those pre-war years. Fred had been working in the village of Cockshutt at Harry Pratt's Blacksmith shop, which was about fifty yards from his home. Why he left Harry Pratt to come to work for me Dad at Welsh Frankton some 8 miles away I never knew. Perhaps there was not the work to keep him in full time employment.

As I sat there quietly, I realised that Fred over the years had been like an elder brother to me. It was Fred who taught me how to mend a puncture in my old pushbike, and also how to fit brake blocks from Joe Butler's Bike Shop in Ellesmere. He also taught me how to light the old carbide light on my bike, not to allow too much water to flow on the carbide.

Fred smoked either Player's or Capstan cigarettes and it was Fred who gave us the 'fag' cards of pictures of famous footballers of yesteryear – Dixie Dean of Everton, Sam Weaver of Newcastle who could throw a football further than some could kick one. A special treat for Christmas was that Fred would buy albums for my brother Frank and me to stick our 'fag' cards in.

One night Fred and I swam Hardwick Pool, but I never

dared to tell my Mother. Then, alas, those balmy days of the 'thirties' came to an end.

I remember one Sunday, my mother told Frank and me to hurry home from Sunday school as someone special was coming to tea. The 'someone' was Fred and he had bought his girlfriend Emily to tea. I expect the bread was sliced thinner than usual, also tins of peaches and cream would be opened as a special treat.

Fred and Emily married soon after and my Dad managed to get them a cottage on Hardwick Estate, the tenancy of No 1 Brow Lane. They occupied that cottage for some sixty odd years. They had two daughters, Ann and Gill. Gill was the one with the pretty frock.

Fred who was in the Ellesmere Fire Service was called up to go to Coventry to fight fires caused by the bombs dropped by the German aeroplanes.

Emily was the first to fail. Fred looked after her for many years, they had by this time moved into a little bungalow in Ellesmere. Emily passed away in Ellesmere Community Centre. Fred also moved there at the age of 92.

I recall how one night in the fifties we took Fred to see his first floodlight football match at Wolverhampton. I can see his face now when the lights came on. Wolves were playing Moscow Dynamo or Spartak or Honved, I can't remember which, but I expect we had the usual pint at The Bucks Head at Wellington and fish and chips at Farmer Giles's shop in Shrewsbury on our way home. Cost of the evening, petrol, tickets, a pint, fish and chips, - and still change out of £3 per person.

When Fred was in his late seventies he used to come to my smithy to make pony shoes for me and the odd spot of blacksmithing about 3 or 4 hours a week. I recall once I said to him "How much do I owe you Fred?" and his reply was: "£4.17.6d. in old money not this damm decimal money"

In 1976, I bought a riding school, saddles, harness, ponies lock stock and barrel. I bought them from Major Halstead and he came to work for me (not many blacksmiths employed a Major!) He came to me one morning and asked if I could find time that day to make and put two front shoes on a horse named Blue. It was essential to put the shoes on that day as Blue was urgently required the next day.

"Leave Blue in the stable tonight," I said.

"I won't be home until after seven" it was a full days shoeing for me "I'll put two shoes on when I get home tonight," I said.

Arriving home late that night, really tired out, I went to the riding school moaning about having to put shoes on a pony after a heavy day's work. But alas there were no ponies in the stables. Cussing under my breath, I thought I'd have to go and catch the damm pony as well, when the phone started to ring in the riding school office. It was Vera, my wife, on the phone to tell me Fred had put the shoes on Blue and also a hind shoe on another pony. Imagine my relief. Fred had probably not put a shoe on a horse for over twenty years. You can never repay that sort of kindness.

The voice of Rev Ann Netherwood, the minister awoke me from my memories of Fred, a friend for some sixty odd years, since he taught me how to mend a puncture with a 9d box of patches and French chalk and valve rubber from Joe Butler's.   .

There doesn't seem to be the Fred Gregory's about today, but I am sure I will find a few more in my writings. I often wonder how many people can remember who taught them how to mend a puncture sixty odd years later. Today in many cases a new tube will be bought, and sometimes even a new bike!

Sequel to a quiet pint

After a fairly busy day I decided to take my grandsons Joe and Tom out for a ride. Their Dad, David also came and we arrived at Llanrhaeadr Water Falls, a local beauty spot. It was about the time the film "The man who went up a hill and came down a mountain" starring Hugh Grant was being made. Quite a lot of people were in Llanrhaeadr, just wandering aimlessly about. We decided to have a drink at one of the local pubs The Hand Inn.

The landlord, Andy Smith greeted us with a smile and after we had ordered our drinks enquired whether we were tourists or locals or just passing travellers.

"We are a bit of everything," David said.

"Well, what part of the country do you come from?" enquired Andy.

"We come from the little village of Welsh Frankton," said David.

"Oh" said Andy, "That's where that village blacksmith who writes books comes from, is he still alive?"

"Yes, I think so," replied David.

Joe could hardly contain himself.

"He's talking about you Grandad," he said.

"I know," I said as I took my drink outside and sat at a table.

"Why don't you tell him, Grandad?" Joe asked.

"Well" I said, "We don't want everyone to know, else my life won't be worth living, crowds will be mobbing me and asking for my autograph, and I won't be able to go anywhere without police protection." I said jokingly!

I could see that Joe still wanted to tell the landlord who I was, and that I was his Grandad.

"Take the empty glasses back," I told Joe, "and you can tell the landlord I will autograph his books for him."

Joe did just that, and when he came back to me he said the landlord said, "Don't go, he is coming out to see you."

When he did appear he shook me by the hand and his remarks made me feel quite proud. He said he thought my books were great and how much he had enjoyed reading them, but they were with his Mother who was reading them so he had not got them with him at the pub, but he would call sometime and get them signed.

I think he did call, and get his books signed.

One sad footnote to this story is; one sunny but cold Sunday afternoon in January 2000 my daughter Valerie took me up to Llanrhaeadr for a ride out. We called for a 'quick pint' at The Hand Inn and with the intention of saying hello to Andy, the landlord, but sadly we were told that he had passed away 2 years previous at the early age of 45. I really was very shocked at this news and would never have thought that one so young and friendly would not be with us today.

The tin bath used by the five brothers on Saturday night with a strong smell of carbolic.

A visit from some American friends

A large mobile motor home pulled up outside my smithy one-day and an American gentleman enquired if I was the guy who wrote books.

"Yes," I replied "But if you don't draw on to the car park you may not live long enough to read them." He parked his mobile home on the car park, got out, shook me by the hand and said: "Gee I sure am glad to see you."
Also with him were his wife and two teenage children.

"Have you got any books that I can buy from you?" he said.

"Certainly," I said, "and would you like to have a look around my blacksmith and farm museum?"

His wife and children got out of their motor home and we all went around my museum. I also showed them the entrance to the escape tunnel, which connects to a cellar in the farmhouse where we lived. The house is possibly 400 years old and for many years was a pub called 'The Green Man' the sign of which hangs in Hardwick Hall, the residence of Col. John Kynaston.

The pub was used not only by the locals but also other dignitaries who came to see the cock-fighting pit which is still in the field just about 30 yards from the house.

Cock fighting is now illegal.

One of the main characters who used to visit was Jack Mytton, the local squire of Halston Hall about a mile away nearer to Whittington. A book has been written about the antics he used to get up to. I believe Nimrod wrote it.

Jack Mytton once had the hiccups, and the story goes on to say that he set fire to his nightshirt to cure them. Also I believe he was rowing his boat on one of his lakes, his wife was with him and he asked her if she was 'his ducky'?

"Yes" she replied.

On that he pushed her into the lake and said "well swim you b."

He also once rode into the dance hall of Halston Hall on the back of a wild bear scattering all the lords and ladies dancing there.

The American gentleman and his family were all fascinated by the stories and the lady asked me if we had found anything interesting inside the escape tunnel leading up to the house.

"Only a Cavalier's hat" I said. I had been pulling their leg, little thinking they would believe me. It was actually my brother Jack's hat, which he had worn when he was in Burma fighting the Japanese with Wingett's Chindits in the 1939-45 war. It looked like the bush hat the Australian Army wore and also the Gurkha soldiers. The lady examined the hat and remarked to me what good condition it was in having been up the tunnel for all those years! She then asked me to sell it to her, but I told her it wasn't for sale at any price, it was a bit of local history. One lie leads to another.

Look after yourself

We had been for a ride with our pony and gig, our two eldest grandsons, Joe Jones and Tom Jones and myself. Joe the eldest, he was about 10 years old and Tom about 8 years old.

Arriving back at Brow Farm the light was fading fast. As we turned into the farmyard Bagel our 14.2 hands high piebald pony was sweating quite a lot as it was a warm sultry evening.

This meant we had to put Bagel into the stable for about an hour or so as she was sweating too much to be turned out into her field, and she needed to have a drink of water, just half a bucket, not too much. She also needed to be rubbed down with wisps of hay from head to tail, all over in fact.

The lads and I did that and then went down to the farmhouse for a drink ourselves. After about an hour or so I decided to take Bagel out to her field, it was quite dark by now.

"Are the lads coming with me?" I asked.

They both decided to come with me. Now Bagel's field is a good half a mile down the main road and up the Perthy road.

Joe walked in front with the torch. After we has put Bagel in her field we decided to come back along the shortcut to Brow Farm, up a very narrow lane saving about 500 yards. The lane is only about 2 feet wide, so there is only room for one person at a time in single file. There are large hedges either side about 12 feet high, the overhanging branches are quite scary. I thought I would have a bit of fun with the lads.

"Who is going to go first?" I asked.

"I will go first Grandad with the torch," Joe said.

"I will come second," I said "And Tom you bring up the rear.

"Oh, and by the way Joe, if you meet a fox or a badger, you shout and then Tom and me can run back"

The wind was whistling in the trees and the lane seemed to be darker than usual. Joe struck off in the front with the torch, I was next and Tom followed close at the rear.

All of a sudden a pigeon or a pheasant flew out of the hedge. It really startled me for a second or so, but we continued on for about another 20 yards or so and then a fox or a badger shot across the path.

"There goes a fox," shouted Joe.

Just at that moment another pheasant startled us with its wings flapping. I felt Tom's feet catching the heels of my boots and with a little fearful cry he said;

"Grandad, can I go in the miggle?"

I suppose he thought he would be safer in the middle – never mind Joe and me!

One of the many elderly visitors to my blacksmith demonstrations –
Mrs. Edwards, aged 91 of Shrewsbury.

Country Education to the fore

We were tidying up our buildings and sorting out any scrap iron that we did not want ready for the scrap lad to fetch. When we were blacksmithing full time we used to have a lot more scrap iron than we do now, and we used to have a rough idea what price we could expect to receive, but with not having so much now I am out of touch with the price of scrap iron. Having said that I can still roughly tell how much weight of scrap iron there is in a 'ruck'

Into the yard with a new wagon arrived the scrap lad; he was not very old.

"Any scrap, Alf ?" he enquired.

"Yes" I said "there is about a ton in a ruck by the shed door"

I knew there was only about half a ton and I knew what his answer to me would be, – and I was right!

"There dunna look much more than 5 cwt" was his reply.

"And also there is a lot of light bars in it."

"O.K." I said, " We will call it half a ton then."

I had not got a clue of the price scrap iron was fetching but I said to him:

"They tell me scrap iron is top price at the moment due to the Gulf War, and that there is a shortage of it because they are making it all into bombs and shells."

"That is the bloody trouble," he said.

"The ships are getting bombed and sunk trying to get out there."

His next remark really made me laugh.

"Another thing is the pound is too strong against the dollar"

Here we were dealing in a few pounds and the fact that

the pound was too strong against the dollar was going to make a big difference to our financial status!

"You can have it for £20" I said.

He walked towards his wagon, got into his driver's seat, switched on the engine and said:

"The best I can do is £10."

"£15," I said "and that's the least I will take."

"O.K." he said, and he backed his wagon up to the scrap and we proceeded to load it on to his wagon, when we were finished I remarked to him.

"You must have nearly a ton on, your tyres are half down."

"No," he said, "I was going to get them blown up at the garage but the air line was out of order."

"Your springs are straight out as well with all the weight," I said to him.

"Yes," he said. They have got to put some stronger springs on for me."

After he had driven out of the yard I thought to myself, there was a lad, with not much education but he had all the answers. And it reminded me of the time when I was buying the chassis off a hearse and the little lad said to me: "it's all right, Mr, it 'anna been driven very fast!"

Gordon Jeffreys who was the head teacher of a local school taught quite a few Romany children. He saw one of the mothers one day and said;

"I taught your son at school"

"You didn'a teach him much" was her quick reply.

No need to, I thought, they were all self educated, common sense.

Another time one of the Romany children was sent to see the Headmaster about something he had done. The school had recently had some new central heating installed and the old cast iron pipes were leaning against the wall, and before the Headmaster had time to say anything the young lad asked him did he want to sell the old piping!

Another time one of them was asked what he would like to make in woodwork class, "clothes pegs" came his reply.

75

Llangollen Eisteddfod

A lady from Ellesmere rang me one evening enquiring if we would be able to accommodate two members of the Polish Girls Choir. This was no problem at all as we had six bedrooms in our old farmhouse and only Vera and I in residence at the time.

The two Polish girls who arrived one evening were students at Warsaw University and were both about 20 years of age.

The first thing that I noticed was the old clothes they were wearing. They were dressed in 'overall' type dresses, very faded but clean. There were patches where they had worn thin.

They chatted for a while in answer to our questions, this proved a little difficult as one of them spoke good English but was unable to understand. The other girl was able to understand English but was unable to speak it well. But we understood enough to know they would like a full English breakfast in the morning.

They were both very tired after travelling and went to bed quite early because they knew a mini bus would be picking them up early next morning to take them to sing at the Eisteddfod at Llangollen.

They taught me how to say 'gin dobry' which translated means 'Good Morning'

That evening they and the rest of the Polish Girls Choir were singing in Ellesmere Parish Church. Vera and I had been invited to go to listen to them along with the other hosts. How different they looked in their national costumes and their singing was first class.

When they had finished singing we waited at the back of the church. As they came down the aisle I greeted them with

'Gin Dobry,' they and all their friends burst out laughing, it was 8 o'clock in the evening and I had just said 'Good Morning!

We took them to the Narrowboat Inn on the side of Shropshire Union Canal for a meal.

German Girls.

We found out from them in broken English that this was a rare treat for them, as meals out were very few in Poland. Also they were not allowed to have chocolate or milk between the ages of six and sixty – and what was sauce? They ate their meal with gusto, sauce and all, out of little individual sachets, and here I made an error. I picked up about six sachets of red sauce and six sachets of brown sauce for them to take back home with them.

I asked one of the girls to open up her handbag and I put

Irish Girls.

the packets of sauce in it and then I said "now run." They were both really frightened after I said that. I suppose the offence of stealing in Poland would mean a severe punishment.

I told Colin Hill, the landlord they were Polish girls and did not have sauce in Poland. On that he went away and came back with an unopened box of sachets of sauce and gave it to them. The look on their faces said it all.

Next morning they were leaving but before they left Jack my brother went to Ellesmere and bought them each a huge bar of chocolate. There were tears in their eyes; it was very emotional to think that a bar of chocolate was such a major treat.

The Berlin Wall came down soon after. I often wonder what happened to the two Polish girls. They gave us a memento; a picture of Chopin inlaid in wood, which still hangs on our living room wall.

The following year we had four Irish girls staying with us, what a difference, they were a laugh a minute. Nothing seemed to bother them; they were younger than the Polish girls about 17 years old.

The next year it was the turn of the German Choir. We were able to take six of them. They were older than the Irish girls, they were very pretty and smart. We were amazed what perfect English they spoke, and when we mentioned this we were told they were taught to speak English at Primary School. It was difficult to get in to conversation with them, they were either shy or more reserved, and did not at any time mention the war.

One thing I do remember quite clearly was their last night with us. They all got dressed up in their national costumes and sang four or five songs just for Vera and me. They looked lovely and their singing was superb. It really was a memorable evening.

The next year we had two older Swedish Ladies, we didn't see much of them, only at breakfast as they used to go out partying and would arrive back at Brow Farm a little worse for wear!

Ah well, it takes all sorts to make the world go round, I often wonder what happened to them all and do they ever remember their stay at Brow Farm, Welsh Frankton, England.

(By the kind permission of Sir J. R. Kynaston, Bart.)

HORDLEY

COURSING MEETING,

On WEDNESDAY, 28th JANUARY, 1863,

STEWARDS:—

I. S. Hodgson, R. C. Edleston, W. W. Cooley and R. G. Jebb, Esquires.

JUDGE... ... ...MR. WARWICK.

HARDWICK CUP.

For Sixteen Dogs, of all ages, at £3 5s. 0d. each.

						£.
The Winner	...	...	...	...	...	28
The Second...	...	...	...	...	...	10
The Third and Fourth, each £3.	...	...	...	...	...	6
Expenses	...	...	...	...	...	8
						52

HORDLEY STAKES.

For Eight Dogs, at £3 5s. 0d. each.

						£.
The Winner	...	...	...	...	...	17
The Second...	...	...	...	...	...	5
Expenses	...	...	...	...	...	4
						26

N.B. Applications to be made to R. G. Jebb, The Lyth, Ellesmere.

Draw &c, at the Green Man Inn, Brow, near Ellesmere, on Tuesday the 27th January, at 4 o'Clock.

MEET AT HORDLEY CHURCH AT HALF-PAST NINE.

BAUGH, PRINTER.

80

Here for the Day

If a school is travelling more than say 30 miles, they usually arrive at my smithy at around 11am. They usually bring a packed lunch with them for their mid-day meal. They have come into the area for the day possibly going on to Llangollen or Oswestry or to the mere at Ellesmere to see all the different kinds of birds that dwell and nest there, or maybe visit the bird sanctuary to see the Herons nesting. A group of children usually stay for about 2 hours, that's one and a half-hours demonstration and then a look around my blacksmith and farm museum. Then we allow about half an hour to have their picnic in the paddock area.

This is a story about a little lass about 9 or 10 years old with blonde hair and done in the old fashioned Shirley Temple ringlets, because it was pouring down with rain it was too wet to have their picnic out of doors so they had to eat their lunch in the Smithy. This little girl had got a packet of crisps for her lunch as well as her sandwiches so I could not help it; I pinched a couple of crisps out of her bag.

The usual letters came from her school saying what they had seen, a horseshoe being made, a poker, a pothook, all things of yesteryear. One little lad had asked Jack when he was making a poker, what is a poker for? How sad I thought, he did not know what a poker was for, a sign of the times, I suppose.

The little blonde girl's letter read something like this:-

Dear Mr Strange,
        Do you remember me, I am the one you pinched a crisp off.

I will never forget her, and the thought went through my head at the time. Gary Lineker gets around £10,000 for the 'pinching crisps' advert, here was one that had it been captured on film, was so natural, no rehearsing – just simply ready made.

I say to every party of schoolchildren when they are leaving don't forget to write to me, and when you get married will you bring your children to see old Alf the Blacksmith.

One little girl aged eleven wrote.

> Dear Alf,
> I will definitely come to see you and I will bring my Grandchildren to see you as well.

I worked it out, I would be about 140 years old by then! The innocence of a young child's mind.

One evening we had a group of aged pensioners to see our demonstrations, they were all getting on a bit and one Granny had bought her eleven year old granddaughter with her. I always ask the question when I am making a horseshoe.

"How many of you have ever seen a horseshoe being made?"

There was only one in the group who put her hand up – the eleven-year-old girl.

I said to her "Where did you see a horseshoe being made?" Her reply was "Here about a month ago!"

A class of sixteen year old girls from a school in the Midlands was booked to come and see my blacksmith demonstration one morning, and what amazed me out of the whole class of about twenty children there was not one white girl amongst them. I could never wish to have a more well behaved class. They asked a lot of interesting questions and they were very interested in what I was doing and in everything I told them.

I always ask every group when they write their letters to me to say what they liked best on their visit to the smithy, and I always have a good laugh when I receive them. One girl wrote:

"It was a cold dark morning, we went into a dark smithy at Mr Strange's, and then suddenly an old man appeared."

(That was me)

One wrote:

"Mr Strange is about as big as my Mum, Mr Strange has got blue eyes, Mr Strange has got brown eyes!!"

I often wonder what 'Me Dad' would have thought of seeing a class of black girls in his smithy. I remember the only black person we saw in our childhood days was when we went on our Sunday School Trips in the 1930's. We would have probably seen a black seaman in the docks as we went through Birkenhead.

To drink or not to drink

(a gallon of water)

On this visit to hospital the majority of patients in this ward had received surgery and part of their treatment was to drink a lot of water every day. As I had only gone in for observations I was not required to drink that much water, however, the nurse in charge of the water jugs did not think that it would do me any harm to take that amount of fluid. Not wishing to upset her I did my best, but alas the quantity of water she wanted me to drink was far too much for me to consume. So every time she came to my bed she gave me a lecture.

Eventually she stopped telling me off about the amount of water I was to drink, except one remark really made me chuckle. "If you want to die, so be it," she said.

When I eventually came home I gave her one of my painted horseshoes for Good Luck, so we parted the best of friends.

83

Panic Stations!!!

More coach companies were now bringing people from as far away as London and Edinburgh and our booking system was getting quite stretched, but being a family concern we were coping quite well, we were also dealing with family run coach companies.

Then at last, (the one and only time) communications broke down. A coach load of Senior Citizens from Liverpool arrived which had not been booked in due to a serious illness of the coach driver's wife who had been rushed to hospital. However, common sense prevailed.

I said to the driver; "If you can take your passengers down to Ellesmere to see the mere for about forty minutes or so, we will then have the Smithy fire lit and ready for your return." This the driver did.

The reason I wanted the people away for about half an hour or so was when you light the Smithy fire a lot of fumes come from the coke and we have to have the two doors open to get the fumes away. This takes twenty minutes or so.

The pensioners arrived back and had a cup of tea and a biscuit and sat on the lawn enjoying their refreshments and then into the Smithy they came. They sat on the old chapel pews ready for my demonstration and talk. There was about fifty of them in the party.

I will have a bit of fun with this lot I thought to myself, I will pull their legs about coming and not being booked in. Aged people from Liverpool I call 'the one liners' as they always seem to have an answer for everything.

"You are a right lot from Liverpool today," I said.

"You made a cock-up of The Grand National, you are trying to get rid of your football manager – Graham Souness, (which they did), and you have made a cock-up of coming to see Alf Strange, The Blacksmith!"

I had hardly finished speaking when one lad in the back row said "Ah, but we did get rid of Derek Hatton."

What the hell Derek Hatton had to do with their trip to Welsh Frankton I do not know but such is the sense of humour of that age group today.

We once had a party from St Peter's School in Liverpool bought to us by Frank Riley, their teacher. They were spending a week on the Trust Boat at Lyneal and were sailing up the Shropshire Union Canal. Frank often called on us with a party of children; they were children who usually had some sort of affliction. This particular day there was a lad of about 14 or so, he was the most deformed child I had ever seen, he sat in the back row of the pews.

"Well," I asked Frank "Who is going to blow the bellows today?"

Immediately, this deformed lad said "Can I Frank, can I blow the fire up today, PLEASE Frank PLEASE."

He really pleaded to be allowed to blow the fire up.

"O.K," said Frank "You can."

He scrambled over the first pew and then fell between the second and third. He got up and then did the same again, throwing himself over the pew and onto the floor. I thought he must have hurt himself and rushed over to help him.

"He will be all right," said Frank "He's used to falling over."

I by now had got hold of him and helped him in his handicapped way to get his hand on the bellows pole. He had to hold onto the wall with his other hand or he would have fallen down again.

He proceeded with great difficulty to blow the fire, it was quite a warm day and after about five minutes he was sweating but he really had got a good fire going.

He then looked at me and said:

"Alf, can I come and work for you?"

I was speechless for a moment and had to turn away from him so that he did not see the tears in my eyes. I will add nothing to that story, only say – "Count your blessings"

85

Another little story that come to mind was the day a young lad of about fifteen years old, in a wheelchair with no legs.

"Alf" he said "Did you hear the story about the two farmers who were falling out."

"No" I said, "I haven't."

"Well" he said "the two farmers were falling out about a horse, the one farmer said, "I thought you told me you gave your horse turpentine."

"Aye," the other farmer said, "I did give my horse turpentine."

"Well," the first farmer said "I gave my horse turpentine and he died."

"Aye, so did mine," the other farmer replied.

We have also had classes of deaf children to see our demonstrations and I am always amazed how quickly the teacher translates my words into sign language, and how swiftly their questions come back!

Metres of Concrete

Another new world that has crept into the farming world, you now order ready-mixed concrete by the 'metre'. One old farming lad did just that but alas they needed 9 or 10 barrow loads to finish the job off. So he decided to measure up himself how much he would require. He wore a size 10 welly he measured one side and then the other side with his size 10 welly.

He rang up to order the concrete, the fellow on the other end of the phone asked him how many metres he required? The old lads reply was "15 welly lengths one side and 11 welly lengths the other side!"

How much was delivered I never found out.

Bristol Crawler?
No – Frankton Plodder!!

As I said in one of my earlier chapters we always give a painted horse shoe, a poker and a pot hook to each party of visitors to use in a raffle, and I always say, no matter what the age group, "Whoever wins the horseshoe it will guarantee fertility" !!

One old lad in the back row who was in his mid eighties said; "Alf, can I have six!" No need for Viagara for him.

Speaking one night to the Three Cocks Vintage Society in Mid Wales, I had been asked to give them a talk about my life as a Village Blacksmith. My talk is based on country characters in and around the Village Smithy.

Dai Evans was the gentleman who asked me to go and talk to them. I had previously bought an Allis B tractor from him, and when I was down in Mid Wales I also bought a Bristol Crawler from him.

As it was in the spring of the year and our busy season of demonstrations was about to begin, I asked him if he could leave it until about October or November when we wouldn't be so busy. He agreed to keep it for me and I was to ring him when I was able to fetch it. Here I repeat the name of it, it was a – "Bristol Crawler" which had tracks on it like a tank – no wheels.

Come October I went to see Ron Jones my best mate who I have previously mentioned in my book. He had bought a new Shogun. I asked him if he would like to give me a ride in it with a trailer behind to fetch the Bristol Crawler. It was a Saturday morning. "All right" he said "We will go down on Monday"

"Fine," I said.

So I rang Dai Evans to tell him we would be coming on Monday

A female voice answered the telephone and I enquired if Mr Evans was in.

"No" she said "I am sorry he is out, can I give him a message?"

"Well" I said "you won't know me, but my name is Alf Strange"

Before I could say anymore she said.

"Oh yes, you are 'THE BRISTOL CRAWLER'

"No" I replied. I am 'THE FRANKTON PLODDER'

She was Dai Evans's daughter and when we eventually met on the Monday morning we had some coffee and sandwiches and we all had quite a laugh about it.

The Bristol Crawler.

A persian cat from Crewe

In the 1930's there was a lad named Bob Jones, who used to come on holiday to Brow Farm where I now live. His Father was a brother to Mr. John Edward Jones who used to live and farm at the Brow. Well his story goes like this. His father Ernie Jones had some marvellous Persian cats, which he used to show. But unfortunately at that particular time in Crewe somebody decided to poison all the cats in that particular area of Crewe. So Ernie Jones asked his brother John Edward could he send his precious Persian cat to stay with him at Brow Farm for a while until they found out who was poisoning all the cats in Crewe.

Crewe was about 30 miles away from Welsh Frankton in those days. The cat was put into a strong carrier bag with a little blanket, and Bob got onto the train at Crewe with the cat. Bob had to change trains at Whitchurch to get a train to Oswestry that stopped at our little village at Welsh Frankton. Bob got off the train at our station and proceeded to walk the mile or so to Brow Farm. About half way there he sensed that something was not quite right in the carrier bag, but his Dad had warned on no account was he to open the bag. He quickened his step and arrived at The Brow just in time to see the 3rd kitten being born to the lovely Persian cat.

So the question still being asked today is, were they Crewe kittens or Frankton kittens? And also another question arose, could they be shown in Shropshire or Staffordshire?

A full list of Silver Cross of St. George winners to date:

Spring 1982: Fiona Hurrell
Derek Howell
Summer 1982: Mary Whitehouse
Autumn 1982: Lord Denning
Zoritza Kasparian
Winter 1982: Capt. Peter Jackson
Dr. Paul Harris
Spring 1983: Alan Keith
Ray Sonin
Summer 1983: Catherine
Bramwell-Booth
Autumn 1983: Mr. Richard Duce
Mrs. Pat Duce
Winter 1983: Dorothy Evans
Dorothy Piddock
Spring 1984: Alf Strange
George Ernest Teal
Summer 1984: George Cushing
Autumn 1984: Barbara Chick
(posthumous)
Winter 1984: Margot Knowles
Len Inwood
Spring 1985: Jack Francis
Reg Adsett
Summer 1985: Raymond Cloud
Autumn 1985: Fred Pettie
Thomas Hodge
Winter 1985: Eric Ball
Harry Mortimer
Spring 1986: Sydney Shaw
Summer 1986: Simon Garrett
Autumn 1986: Andrew Millar
Winter 1986: Arthur Dalby

The Silver Cross of St. George was first awarded in our Spring 1982 issue, since when 88 have been presented to a wide variety of men and women at home and abroad in recognition of their spirit and enterprise in preserving England's traditions and promoting the English way of life.

Spring 1987: Robert Boldys
Summer 1987: George Stafford
Autumn 1987: Hilda Maidment
Winter 1987: Father Kenneth
Loveless
Spring 1988: Eric Fayne
Summer 1988: Leslie Coe
Autumn 1988: Mrs. Alwyn Law
Winter 1988: Nelson Owen
Spring 1989: Anthony Cooney
Summer 1989: Stanley Long
Autumn 1989: Dame Thora Hird
Winter 1989: Margaret Watson
Ken Garfoot
Norman Williams
Ernest Sykes

Veronica Huthwaite
Rose Morris
Spring 1990: Jonathan Hall
Summer 1990: Dr. Margaret and
Dr. Anthony Barker
Autumn 1990: Evelyn Appleyard
Winter 1990: Winnie Bristow
Spring 1991: Margaret Thatcher
Summer 1991: Lis Dorer
Autumn 1991: John Arlott
Winter 1991: Josephine Butler
Spring 1992: Major Ross Watson
Summer 1992: Sara Marojica
Autumn 1992: Enoch Powell
Winter 1992: John Minshull-Fogg
Spring 1993: Anita Goulden

Summer 1993: Five MPs representing all the anti-federal Europe rebels on both sides of the House of Commons:
Nicholas Budgen
William Cash
Austin Mitchell
Peter Shore
Sir Teddy Taylor
Autumn 1993: Bobby Charlton
Winter 1993: Norman Hunter
Spring 1994: Hilda White
Summer 1994: Gordon
Beningfield
Autumn 1994: The Right Rev.
Nelson Burroughs
Dr. Otto G. Tucker
Winter 1994: Colin Cook
Spring 1995: Crispin Beale
Summer 1995: Elizabeth Lucas
Harrison
Autumn 1995: Elizabeth Balfour
Winter 1995: Dorothy Melby
Spring 1996: Anne Mallinson
Summer 1996: Peter Dunstan
Autumn 1996: John Foster
Winter 1996: Peter Glossop
Spring 1997: Vice-Admiral Sir
Louis Le Bailly
Peter Sandell
Summer 1997: Roland Smith
Autumn 1997: Cherie Goode
Winter 1997: Lord Tonypandy
Sir James Goldsmith
(both posthumous)

Roll of Honour

The Silver Cross of St. George was first awarded in 1982, since when 88 have been awarded to a wide variety of men and women at home and abroad in recognition of their spirit and enterprise in preserving England's tradition and promoting the English Way of Life.

How long in the public eye?

After the rebuilding of my village smithy and reconstructing it back to what it was like 200 years ago coach loads of senior citizens were beginning to come from further afield than Shropshire. They were arriving from Birmingham, London Edinburgh and many other places in between.

In 1984 we received an award from This England Magazine for what we had done to further the English way of life.

The Silver Cross of St George was first awarded in the spring of 1982 issue. Since then 88 have been awarded to a wide variety of men and women at home and abroad in recognition of their spirit and enterprise in preserving England's tradition and promoting the English way of life.

Only four Crosses of St George are awarded each year in Spring, Summer, Autumn and Winter issues. Occasionally though, in special circumstances five or six are awarded.

In the spring edition of 1998 there was a roll of honour which contained all the names of people who had received this award. I felt very proud and honoured to be in such illustrious company of so many famous people. I showed the list to my daughter-in-law Catherine and asked her to show it to her children and to tell them what a famous Grandfather they have.

I told her to point out that I won the award in 1984, and that Bobby Charlton won it nine years later in 1993.

Next morning I enquired what the children thought of me winning the award before Bobby Charlton, the famous Manchester United footballer, her answer was that David her eldest son who was 11 years old said; "Who is Bobby Charlton?" (And by the way young David is a Manchester United supporter!

He would probably remember Gazza or Michael Owen but in nine years you are forgotten. – Ah Well !!

Clayton Jones – Poet

In 1935 Clayton Jones wrote the annual piece of poetry for me to recite. He wrote about the education at Ellesmere College, a fee-paying private school.

Ellesmere College is still going strong, and has become very well known. John Brunt distinguished himself in the 1939-45 war, by being awarded the highest military medal for bravery beyond the course of duty, the Victoria Cross.

Also Bill Beaumont was a former student of Ellesmere College. He later became Captain of the England Rugby Team.

It is over sixty-five years since the late Clayton Jones wrote his poetry about Ellesmere College, and in another thirty five years bringing us up to the year 2035 I guess the college will go from strength to strength and produce many more outstanding students.

I see Ellesmere College every time I go outside my home as it is only about a mile away, as the crow flies.

After he wrote about the college he went on to say;

"How we are fixed up Frankton way, the same seven days goes to the week – that's 14 milkings so to speak."

He goes on to say "We wouldn't mind three times a day if the Market Board would rise the pay, because the price paid is just an insult to the cow."

Over the last sixty years, cows have gone from being milked by hand, someone sat on a milking stool and using a milk bucket, to being milked by a machine. By pressing a button the correct amount of corn is supplied to each cow, and on many farms milking three times a day is common. But still farmers complain and in many cases rightly so. Recently a farmer told me his milk cheque was £1300, but his corn bill was £1000 so there was about £300 left to pay his rent, wages, community charge, diesel and oil for his tractor and running the car.

Clayton Jones wrote "With everything all nice and quiet, nothing much to cause a riot." I wonder what his words would be today over sixty years later, when petrol has been averaging over £4 a gallon and milk less than £1. So would he still be able to write the difference in price. It is still an insult to the cow.

In 1935 he wrote –

> What do you think of our new bus?
> A right good thing for most of us
> Who canna run a motor car
> Or push an owd bike far
> The new bus is a decent ride,
> That is a fact Tom canna Hide.

The wit in that last line is the fact that the man who bought the bus was called 'Tom Hyde'

Today most households own a car, in lots of cases two or even three cars, so most of us can run a car. Petrol in the 1930's would be about one shilling and sixpence a gallon, today in the early 2000's it is over £4, yet today we can on average run two cars per family.

> Some says we've got a station,
> But why its there just beats creation,
> 'cos its built behind a wicket,
> Out in the wilds down by Crickett.
> So when we travels most of us,
> We walks or bikes or gets the bus.

Alas, Frankton station closed in the late fifties, so ending the link from Crewe to Oswestry also the transport to Oswestry on a Wednesday for a lot of Frankton people. With hindsight and with the present price of world oil, and if trains were still fired by coal, of which our country has plenty of, perhaps it was a backward step to disband them and remove the rails that the trains ran on.

Also there is the plight of the overloaded motorways and the pollution of the environment which now seems to be on everyone's lips and the government is now banning leaded petrol. One wonders what we are leaving for our Grandchildren and future generations to inherit. It is called progress.!

Many households knew what time it was when they heard the sound of the train.

Today Frankton station is an agricultural depot and is currently for sale for just under £200,000.

Gone also are the likes of Mr Berwick the Stationmaster and a porter named Les Almond.

Gone alas are the days when we could go down there on our bikes and race around the tarmac yard and skid on the loose chippings, and if you had any money a penny bar of chocolate could be had from the big red chocolate machine or a 'tuppenny' packet of woodbines out of the fag machine.

Dare we forecast that in the year a hundred years after Clayton Jones wrote of the folly of having a railway station out in the wilds? Will it maybe have a helicopter pad for Japanese golfers to land and play golf at the Brow Golf course, as the Brow Golf course helicopter pad is over used. I wonder how far out that forecast will be. Who knows!

He wrote about the plight on the barges on the canal "because a cut barge cannot hurry as quickly as a motor lorry, and that Frankton Port basin won't make a fool of Bristol, Hull or Liverpool."

Many millions of pounds are being spent on the Waterways of Great Britain and once again it will be possible to come and go by canal boat from Yorkshire to Newtown in Mid Wales. The locks at Lower Frankton will once again become a hive of activity as more boats are put on the canals, moorings appearing every few miles, houses bordering the canalside will be changed into pubs and eating places. More and more tourists arriving from all over the world and one wonders will it not be long before traffic lights will be appearing at the busy parts of the canals. And one wonders how long it will be before 'canal rage' appears in the courts.

But at least traffic would be taken off the busy congested roadways of Great Britain and council workers will be directed to operate the canals. Think of the money that would be saved paying Highway Officials never mind the saving of salt and sand that is sometimes put on the roads. There would be no need for salt and sand on the canals, and one wonders what would happen to all the money that would be saved. I am sure that there would be some over-educated official who would come up with some idea. I wonder how far out this forecast will be in the year 2035.

When I look back at that piece of poetry written some sixty odd years ago and one lets one's pen and mind wander, it is quite frightening really how true a lot of forecasts can be, and also how some of them can be miles out. The truth is that life really is very short and as one's mind wanders back to those old school days they seem like only yesterday. I have been a pensioner for nearly ten years and when one looks back to when we were teenagers, people in their fifties seemed old, and then in no time at all we are pensioners ourselves.

Clayton Jones wrote about being in bed by 8 o'clock at night. It is not unusual for me to be giving an after dinner speech some 50 or 60 miles away from Welsh Frankton, starting to talk at 9 – 9.30.pm and then to drive home, and then to do the same thing again a couple of nights later.

The building up of a Museum

Having now got my smithy looking as if it was over 150 years old, the chapel pews to seat seventy people and my Granddad's anvil, the one that Granny Strange sat on to test how much work had been done. This was the time to start to buy old implements etc. for another building that we wanted to bring into use. One corner of the building was made into an old fashioned kitchen of yesteryear, with an old black leaded grate and a hip bath that had come from our old home.

The rest of the building is filled with old household pieces; I acquired lots of memorabilia. People from as far away as 50 miles would ring up, "Alf, come and look at what we have got to sell." Invariably the husband had passed away, possibly a farmer, who when they had retired had moved into a little cottage with a few acres of land. An old workshop-cum-shed would be a must. Off I would go to see what they had got for sale, often as not you would have a job to get into the place.

"Well," I would say "and what have you got in there?"

"Only God knows," in many cases would be the answer.

"All I know he (meaning her husband) used to spend a lot of his spare time in this 'owd shed mending one thing after another."

"How much do you want for all the contents?" I would ask.

"Well, whatever you give me will go to Cancer Research, or The British Heart Foundation or some other worth cause," would be their reply. They knew that I would put them under cover or on show for other people and children to look at and enjoy.

Sometimes there may be about £50 worth in there.

The Demonstration Smithy.

"£50" I would say.

"Right" would be their reply, or £30 if it was not such a big shed!

I was never very far out in my estimate, and I can honestly say I have never found any gold watches or diamond rings in any lot that I have bought. Occasionally people will bring me things like old hay knives, brushing hooks, wet stones etc. and I have always tried to find out if there is any little story attached to any of the bits and pieces. Did they belong to a country character, did he or she have a country saying? Over the years I have built up quite a few interesting stories, some true and some you take with a pinch of salt, but as in most of my stories there is always a little bit of truth, I may add a bit or take away a bit, so I am now going to tell you a few stories about the implements.

The first story concerns a turf or peat barrow, I acquired it from Fenn's Bank and it was the last turf barrow to be used for the carrying of turf. It is similar to a porter's barrow on railway stations.

Turf at one time used to be cut and stacked in rucks like bricks and left to dry for a period of time, piles would be over an area of land which belonged to a smallholder. After it had dried sufficiently it would then be loaded on to a horse drawn cart and sold around the North Shropshire area.

Later motor lorries came along. Many loads of turf were bought by my Dad for the hooping of wheels before the 1939-45 war, he would sometimes shoe a horse in exchange for a load of turf.

Then sometime in the late seventies, men moved into the Fenn's Bank, Whixhall area with bulldozers and diggers and for want of a better word would rape the land and would take more turf out in one day than a smallholder would take out in possibly a year. Then there was a Act of Parliament in the late eighties or early nineties which said that no more turf was to be taken from Fenns or Whixhall Moss as it was lowering the water table and affecting the environment – a word that is quite commonly used.

Gooseberries and Custard!!

Before the 1939-45 war the collection of household rubbish etc. was not even heard of. I suppose there was not so much pre-packed food back then. Tins, bottles and glass jars were usually put into a pre-dug hole either in the woods or in the corner of a field or garden. Collection by a dustcart or what we to-day call a scavenge wagon was unheard of in the country villages; only the towns had this luxury service, nowhere for them to tip their rubbish.

The reason I am writing about this is that a few years ago whilst walking through our Brow Wood looking at the bluebells I spotted a glass jar just below the surface of the ground. On inspection I found a kilner jar still perfectly sealed full of gooseberries, which I imagine were bottled by some members of Welsh Frankton W.I. in about 1940, saving food to help out meagre rations. What it was doing in the wood I don't know. Perhaps someone cleaning out one of their cupboards after the war thought they would have been of no use. However sixty years after they were picked and bottled, they are displayed in the old fashioned kitchen in my museum and look in perfect condition.

Just recently a local craftsman has given me a sealed tin of Symington's custard powder, also in perfect condition, which I suppose is also about sixty years old. He had found it in the cupboard of an old house he was renovating.

The tin of custard powder and the jar of gooseberries are now standing side by side. Only the other day a lady who was on a visiting coach party asked me when I was going to open them?

I thought for a moment and then I said "I will open them for tea, I will open them in the millennium."

Gooseberries and custard! I think they would have the same effect as a good dose of my Mother's castor oil. !!

Fenn's Bank last Turf Barrow

Many years ago I went to Fenn's Bank and there were lots of turf barrows there when they were being used by smallholders, but when I went to buy one they had all disappeared, all except one which Jack found in an old shed. We bought it home and did a few repairs to it and put it in my museum. When I tell people who visit my museum that it is the last turf barrow from Whixhall Moss no one has yet disagreed with me, maybe one day someone will.

Now the story about it;

I was told when I fetched it that two Irish lads who had been made redundant had used it. As there was very little work in the North Shropshire area they both decided to emigrate to Australia. I cannot remember their names but I will call them Pat and Mike. Australia is a very difficult country to emigrate to due to various regulations and rather strict rules.

Pat went in first to see the immigration official and the first question he was asked was what his trade had been in North Shropshire?

Pat replied that he had been a 'pilot'

"A pilot," said the immigration official.

"Just sign this form and you can be in Australia in a few days, we are very short of 'pilots' in Australia, send your mate Mike in to see me now."

This Pat did.

"Right" said the official, "Mike, what do you do for a living?"

"I am a turf cutter," said Mike.

"Oh dear" said the official, "I am sorry but there is no work for you here, we do not need any turf cutters in Australia."

"But you have just let my mate Pat in," said Mike.

"Yes" said the official "but he is a 'pilot.'

"Yes" said Mike "but if I am not there to cut the turf, he canna' bloody pile it" !!

The old tin bath on the hearthrug in my old re-constructed kitchen in my museum is one that my four brothers and I used to have a bath in every Saturday night, whether we needed one or not.

The hot water was one from the old fashioned coal and stick boiler, and there was always a clean grey flannelette shirt to change in to.

White shirts were only worn for Chapel on Sunday and Sunday school in the afternoon. Our shoes were black and polished and we wore long grey socks and short grey trousers – no long trousers until you left school.

Last Turf Barrow.

Mast Foreman – Girl of 25

Changing times in a modern world. A new 4 x 4 wheel drive vehicle drove into our farmyard and out of it stepped a smartly dressed young man aged about 24. He enquired who owned the fields at the back of one of our old farm buildings. I was able to tell him that it was I. He then asked me if I minded if he took some levels of the ground as they were looking for somewhere in this area to put up a Telecommunications mobile Telephone Mast. They had chosen this area as we are about 600 feet above sea level. We went to the back of our Old Dutch Barn to where there is a piece of rough ground not suitable for farming. "This will be ideal," he said.

"I will come back next week with our crane and driver and provided we can see Wrexham Police Station, high ground at Whitchurch, Telford and Oswestry from this point we would be interested in putting up a mast and tower here, for which we would pay you a rent for the piece of ground, to be reviewed every 3 years for the next 20 years."

The crane, complete with its driver, arrived the following Monday morning at about 8 o'clock. It was very foggy that particular morning which meant the crane driver could not do anything as the visibility was so poor. In fact it was very foggy for the next four days, and I believe the crane and its driver were costing something like £500 per day.

However the levels were suitable and a price was to be arranged between a solicitor and an auctioneer, this was taken out of my hands. Eventually everything was agreed and a date to commence work was arranged.

Lorry loads of material started arriving, it looked as if they were going to put up a new Forth Bridge, never mind a telephone mast. Girders and angle irons, nuts and bolts were everywhere, how to sort that lot out was beyond me. Soon after, another 4 x 4 wheel drive vehicle arrived, out of which stepped a very smart young lass of about 22 or 23 years of age. The young man then made a remark which really surprised me.

"Mr Strange" he said, "This is the foreman who will be in charge of the site for the next month or so."

She shook me by the hand and introduced herself as Alish, to which I replied "Well, my name is Alf, I prefer that to Mr Strange."

"Right, Alf" she said. "I have arranged a site meeting in the morning at 9 o'clock and I would like you to attend, please." I thought to myself, What the hell do I know about mobile phones and telephone masts! "All right" I said, "I will be there"

Dead on 5 to 9 she arrived having travelled up from Crewe some thirty miles away. There was already about 8 or 10 men waiting to meet her. She introduced herself to the men, shook each one by the hand and enquired their names. She then introduced me to them all saying "This is Alf, who owns the site, and if you want anything you only have to ask him and he will be only too glad to help you if he can. Please don't take things for granted."

I looked at all of the men and I knew immediately that she had got their respect and support.

The next 3 weeks or so went with a swing, if Alish was not here, work was still being done just the same, no slacking off. I believe I am right in saying that the mast was finished 3 or 4 days ahead of time. My mind went back to my early days and my recollection of site foremen. They always seemed to require slaves and were always shouting at the men. I thought what a lot we had to learn. Here was a young lass in charge of about 3 different sites and yet always arriving with a smile on her face.

Another lesson learned, treat everyone as you would expect to be treated yourself.

Take not the life you can give, because everything has a right to live!

Those few lines were said to me as a lad some 60 odd years ago walking along our bottom road to reach one of our fields.

Mrs Jarvis of No 4 Higher Perthy was the lady who spoke those words to me. I had got my first catapult and was going to try and get us a rabbit for our dinner. Anyone who does not know what a catapult is, it is like a sling with a forked stick which has a piece of elastic and a piece of leather to hold a stone or a $\frac{1}{2}$ inch nut in.

You then aim the forked piece of wood at the rabbit, pull back the elastic loose go of the piece of leather and the stone would be launched at great speed hopefully towards the rabbit. If you hit the rabbit in the head, rabbit pie for dinner the next day; if you missed, away would go the rabbit down the hole in the ground to its burrow.

Jack Haynes and Brother Jack would often go and get a couple of rabbits with a double barrel shotgun on their way home after a night on duty in the home guard in the Parish Hall.

Then one day disaster struck Jack Haynes was called up into the Airforce, and Brother Jack to the Army R.A.Corp. It was now left to me in 1942 to get a supply of rabbits for our kitchen table, a job I did not relish after thinking about Mrs Jarvis's two lines of poetry. But self-survival took over and having seen lots of rabbits caught in gin traps I should imagine death by a shotgun was much better than being trapped by the legs for up to two days in a snare.

A rabbit pie or rabbit stew was the staple diet for most country homes through the war years and into the fifties. And then in my opinion man inflicted the most terrible disease

104

called myxamatosis to try and control the population of rabbits. A few rabbits were infected with the disease then let loose in different parts of the country and then in what seemed like no time at all rabbits were nearly extinct. Hundreds of acres of land with hardly a rabbit in sight. It would be nothing to walk into a field and have to kill about 10 rabbits or so to put them out of their suffering. It was a terrible disease; it was like a flu except their heads would swell up, their eyes would bulge and they would go blind. You would find them just sitting there waiting for either dog or man to put them out of their misery. But, of course, it was better for farming, more grain, better crops. Acres of land which only seemed to keep rabbits now came back into production, some producing 3 tonnes to the acre.

Why I have chosen to write these few lines is to bring me on to something that is very much to the fore and on everyone's lips at the moment, more in the country than in the towns – the banning of fox hunting with hounds not dogs.

Now I do not like cruelty to animals in any shape or form, and I do feel that man is playing with nature whereby certain species of predators are allowed to live and not controlled nature, if left alone would level things out. I being a Countryman born and bred think the control of foxes at the moment is much less cruel than by shooting, snaring or poisoning. And having seen a fox suffering a lingering death through being shot, possibly weeks before lead poisoning put him out of his misery. Also I have seen foxes with three legs having been snared and then bitten through its own legs to release itself from the snare. Or to find one hit by a motor car left to die in the middle of the main road with its back broken, possibly by an anti-hunt person too busy to stop and check if the fox were dead or not.

I recall a knock one evening on our front door by a person who had just hit a fox asking if I could help her. The fox was very badly hurt and was going to die. I pulled the fox to the side of the road and fetched an old type policeman's truncheon, and with one swift blow to the back of its head put the poor fox out of his misery. I was then accused by the other person of being cruel and heartless, Ah well it takes all sorts.

Having once had over 3 dozen point-of-lay pullets with their heads bitten clean off, one sometimes has to control one's own temper with regards to the fox's wanton killing. The killing for the sake of it. The pullets were from Hulson Chick Farm at Whixhall.

On part of our farm we have developed a 9-hole golf course. The field we developed lends itself ideally for the purpose being und ·lating terrain. We have planted hundreds of trees and left some ı ∪ugh areas for all sorts of wildlife. We also developed two old ponds by enlarging them thus making them into water hazards on the fairways. We made a large island in the middle of one of them with the hope that one of the many water hens or ducks would maybe nest there. We were fortunate enough to get two ducks to do just that, and what a lovely sight it was when the eggs hatched out to see nine little ducklings on one pool and 10 on the other. But, alas, nature can be so cruel. Within a week or ten days not one little duck remained. The hawk had taken them all just the odd legs or piece of wing left as evidence. The hawk is a bird of prey, a protected species.

Talking to an anti-hunt supporter one morning all of a sudden he said to me: "What is that magpie doing?"

"Oh" I said. "He is just looking for his breakfast in the top of the hedgerow." Sure enough it was not long before out he came with a young bird out of the nest and devoured it in no time at all. He said, "That's cruel," but I replied: "That's nature, man is playing with the balance of nature. If we left it to look after itself things would keep themselves in prospective."

"So why hunt the fox?" he asked.

I replied, "If man did not hunt the fox. In a few years time, the fox could possibly become extinct due to shooting, poisoning and snaring," as I have already mentioned. When the hounds catch a fox and very few are caught as they are very clever animals, hence the saying 'as sly as an old fox', death is virtually instantaneous.

One of the true facts of life is, were fox hunting to be banned it would put an awful lot of people out of work. Only recently I was talking to a farrier who would have to make two out of the four men who worked for him redundant. I would like to say here and now, that people who do not know anything about nature should leave well alone, and let nature look after itself.

I am not a particularly religious person, but I do claim to be a Christian, so I now repeat –

"Take not the life you cannot give"

"Because everything has a right to live."

These are my own personal thoughts, as thankfully we still live in a society with freedom of speech. I might also add that I have many friends on both sides of the argument.

Late night shopping has a twist!

Vera wanted a few things one evening so she could finish making a wedding cake. We decided to nip down to the late night supermarket just down the road at Park Hall by the old army camp.

As usual it was raining and blowing a gale so I said to Vera I would sit here in the car and wait for you. Now as most of you know when you go in to supermarkets these days they always have brightly coloured posters advertising what they have on 'Special Offer' for that particular week. Cod pieces so much, margarine half price, 'buy one – get one free' etc. In the middle of all the special offer posters was a little notice which read. "Come to Whittington Ladies Club this Friday night and listen to a talk given by our local blacksmith – Alf Strange."

Under this little notice some bright spark had added the words –

"This weeks 'special offer' A Battered Blacksmith!!"

The Olympic Games – 1948

The name of Fanny Blankers-Kohn was a household name in 1948. She was I believe the Olympic Champion in her event when the games were held in London just after the 1939-45 war.

She was of Dutch descent and was a famous runner of that era.

What connection you may ask has that to do with my memoirs. Well like many of my stories, sequels have a sequel.

A few years ago we had a coach party of Senior Citizens from somewhere, I can't quite remember where, and in the visiting party was a rather frail looking little old lady, she was, if I remember right, using a walking frame. I got into conversation with her and she told me that she had been in the Army at Park Hall Camp just the other side of Whittington about 4 miles away

She had been in the A.T.S. a very famous Corps. where thousands of Army Recruits had done their training for the 1939-45 war with Germany.

She herself was a runner and had done her training on the athletics track at Park Hall, and her claim to fame was that in the trials she ran second to Fanny Blanker-Kohn, and with a smile on her face she added that she was only 'a yard or two' behind her at the finish!

I thought then what a cross section of people I have come to see my blacksmith demonstrations and me. Who would have thought seeing her on her walking frame that was the story that she had to tell? As I have said many times if you live to get old, old age does not come alone, but you cannot take our memories from us.

Sadly I forgot to ask her name, but hopefully if any of her family read this they will know who I mean.

The day we nearly held up Royalty

Many years ago, Sgt Jervis from Ellesmere Police called to see me to inform me that a certain member of the Royal Family was going to open a new part of the world famous Orthopaedic Hospital at Gobowen. The Royal Party would be passing our farm at approximately 11 o'clock the following morning. Apparently she was arriving at Shawbury airfield at about 10.15.am. and then going on to the hospital, which is where patients from all over the world come for specialist treatment for bone complaints and surgery.

The majority of the land of Brow Farm, about 70 acres, is situated the other side of a very busy main road. The farmhouse, farm buildings and about another 30 acres of land on this side, the wrong side if you like, it should have been the other way around which would have meant not so many journeys across a very dangerous stretch of road. Also with a blind hill about 50 yards from the farm gate, cars and lorries etc. come over the top at about 70mph with very little hope of stopping should anything or anybody be in the way. I must say, vex or please, it is a very dangerous place to live. The police say it is a dangerous spot, all the various Road Safety Committees agree, but sadly the people from the Highways Department who could do something about it are no help at all. Why, I just do not know.

But I must get off this subject now or I may make some libelous remark.

Now back to the visit of Sgt Jervis whose request was that could I not be on the road with my little 'Fergie' tractor and muck-spreader between 11 and 12 o'clock and also that their Royal Highnesses would be travelling back between 3 and 4 o'clock in the afternoon. Quite a lot of the local Frankton residents came to Brow Farm to watch her go past. The chauffeur slowed their Rolls Royce or was it a Daimler with the Royal Standard on the front right down and she waved to us all.

Ian our herdsman at the time took a load of manure across the road to spread on the fields. We then put another load on the spreader ready to be taken across the road later in the afternoon after HRH had gone back. At about 3 o'clock the cavalcade of police motorbikes and police cars went by so I went to the top of the Brow to slow the traffic down enabling Ian to cross the road with tractor and muck-spreader. Ian was waiting for me to give him the signal to cross the road when on looking towards Oswestry I couldn't believe my eyes, another Police car and Police motorbikes all with blue lights flashing. Behind them was the big black Daimler with the Royal Standard on the front. I realised immediately who it was and went to the middle of the road to wave to Ian to tell him to wait. He thought I was waving him across the road, at the same time the Police car and the Royal car accelerated, too late for me to stop them or do anything about the situation. A quick prayer to the Almighty must have worked for Ian managed to get across the road just in time as the cars swept by. Why they were later than the first set of police cars and motorbikes probably by a good 10 minutes or so I just do not know.

Little did they know how close they came to a load of muck, and I wonder if they would have damaged my little 'fergie' tractor and could I have made a claim on their insurance!

Talking to Sgt Jervis some time later he remarked on how well the day had gone with no problems – little did he know how close a call she had with a muck-spreader, and possibly how close Ian and I had come to the Tower of London. Just another little memory of yesterday.

Was it fate that 12 months later whilst fetching a pig in a trailer from Whitehurst by Chirk a similar incident occurred.

Oh No! Royalty again

I had bought some in pig gilts off a Mr Morris, a farmer from Whitehurst, the other side of Chirk. At that time the only transport we had was a clapped out old Landrover and a very dilapidated old trailer, towed by the old Landrover. Side mirror, brakes and a dropper pin with a cotter pin to stop the draw pin from coming out. We were going to go the back way to the other side of Chirk. Down past Harold Edward's at Pen y Bryn and on nearly in to Whitehurst, turn right by G Stevenson blacksmith shop, now a petrol station, and on to Mr Morris's farm. We were not to know that Royalty was at Llangollen that particular day.

After loading the pig in to the trailer with the old type net over the top to stop her jumping out we set off home. We decided to stay on the main road and go through the middle of Chirk instead of taking the back roads home. We were greeted by cheering crowds which were lining the street, we were apparently just ahead of Royalty – again.! They had been visiting the International Eisteddfod at Llangollen.

The pig had somehow or other managed to stand on her hind legs, with her front feet resting on the front board of the trailer and she was viewing the crowds as if she was 'Royalty' herself.

What speed we were doing when we came past Ron Wilson's pub The Bridge Inn, at the bottom of Chirk Bank I dread to think. Ron Wilson was one of my old school mates. As luck again was on my side we got to the cross roads at Gledrid and quickly decided to take a detour through St Martins, New Marton, Lower Ridge, Higher Ridge and home to the Perthy blacksmith shop.

We possibly left our hour of glory behind us, and we

didn't even get a mention in the local paper The Oswestry Advertizer, but this did happen in a lifetime.

As the old saying goes, "Better to be born lucky than rich" But rich are the memories of yesteryear.

The Church and School at Welsh Frankton

Summary of a long hand account made by the first incumbent of the separate parish of Welsh Frankton. (Sro/4288p par 1)

The late Rector of Whittington, the Rev. C. A. A. Lloyd, first rented a building which was licensed for divine service in 1835 to counteract the effect of the building of the Dissenting Meeting House near by. It was first opened for service on St Andrews Day Monday, 30th November 1835, a certain Robert Montgomery being Mr Lloyd's curate at the time.

This licensed building was most rudely and roughly finished and fitted and merited the happy name given to it by the Squire of Whittington parish, The consecrated cowshed. It was frequently spoken of as 'the Bottle Chapel' from the sight of the public house opposite. It was built on the old school with sliding doors which were opened in service time and continued to be used till the consecration of the present church 9.8.58.

The old school to which the old chapel was added some years after was built by the Rector of Whittington Mr Lloyd, upon the site which he had purchased in 1824. It was a small brick building very low pitched but well adapted for the purpose for which it was built.

The old school and the chapel were pulled down and the present school erected on the site of the old chapel to the design of E Haycock the architect. It was opened 14.2.1863. The cost was £425.17s 11d.

Alf Strange – Blacksmith

I visited a smithy last night, Alf Strange was the Blacksmith's name,
He told us tales about his life as he took us down 'Memory Lane'
He showed us the very can he had used, to make the chippies their
    tea,
Mornings it was half past ten, afternoons it was quarter past three.

We heard the tales from long ago, how hard they had worked and
    how long,
And as Alf shaped a horseshoe, the anvil rang its song.
The Reverend Bert stood ready and well the bellows blew,
As Alf with his brother Jack the striker, struck holes through the
    horses shoe.

Down from the walls strange shoes were unhooked, shaped for
    horses with corns and in pain,
Alf showed us another aged 600 years which under a field had lain,
Then with a long straight rod of hot iron, and the art and skill of
    his trade,
He teased and shaped that long straight rod and a poker and 'S'
    hook were made.

We heard the story of Miss Salter's crop and the golf Alf missed one
    day,
She ran out of petrol and her car it did stop, so with Grandfather's
    crop did she pay,
Alf spoke of all the folk he had met and the 'Country Education'
    he'd had
Stories about his Granny and his Dad long remembered since he
    was a lad.

A horseshoe now hangs on my kitchen wall, painted by Alf's lady
    wife,
When I look at it I always remember:-
    The Smithy, A Strange Blacksmith's Life. !!!

My Life

by a railway container

Little did I think when I was growing as a tree in a wood what life awaited me. Tree Fellers came into the wood and I was selected to be sawn down, cut into lengths, then lugged away on a large lorry and eventually arrive at a large saw mill to be sawn into planks of a certain length and left to dry out for a year or two. Then again loaded onto a wagon and transported again to a Railway Workshop to be again cut up into various lengths and made into a railway container. Iron wheels were then put on two large girders which formed the bottom of me. Then again transported to a Railway line to become another L.M.S. Railway container to travel the length and breadth of the British Isles.

For many years life was very boring really, racing up and down the country from one town to another, shunted into various railway sidings, loaded up with this and that and then one day I with several others was shunted into a Railway siding and left there for many years. What was to become of us we used to ask one another, were we going to be chopped up and burned, "sold for scrap" said another and then the day dawned.

Quite a few of us were bought by a Mr. Tudor Griffiths of Ellesmere Agriculture Ltd. The four wheels had been taken off and so we went through a lovely part of the Country on the back of a big transporter to Ellesmere, past Ellesmere to Wood Lane Gravel Hole. Again we stayed there for quite a while until one day some men came to look us over, prodding with nails and knives to see if we were rotten. I must have been in good condition for I was bought and transported 2 miles to a lovely place called Hardwick Park, Welsh

Frankton. I was placed in the shade of a large tree but I could see the stately Hardwick Hall.

Again men approached and I was partitioned off into two compartments and seats were made all around the inside of me and then it dawned on me what I was now to be. Because one Saturday afternoon 22 men arrived all dressed up in white trousers and white sweaters. I was now Welsh Frankton Cricket Club Pavilion – what a change from tearing up and down the country.

"The Board Room."

I quite enjoyed the summer months especially Thursday evenings Bill, Arthur and Albert came and hoards of children came to practice. Quite a nice part of my life and one lad whose name was Andrew Lloyd went up to play for Warwickshire and England. The worst part of being a cricket pavilion was the winter months, very lonely except for the odd courting couple and a visit from the odd fox or men

116

went by with shot guns, pheasant shooting parties, and then spring would come again the same routine.

After about 15 years I guessed something else was going to happen to me. More meetings than usual were being held in me, and then it happened, I was to be sold and replaced by a new pavilion. Again loaded onto a tractor and unceremonially dumped on a concrete yard, Alf's farm, what a contrast. Traffic belting up and down the brow day and night, no peace at all not a bit like the quiet lane of Hardwick Park which I can still see out of my own windows. Not in my wildest dreams did I realise what a change of life style I was going to have for the next 30 years. Not much happened for two years, I was just used as a strong shed for Alf. "Chuck it in the shed" were the words I heard very often. "The shed" I ask you and then a day I shall never forget came.

For a few weeks I had been the home of some young calves. Foot and mouth disease was in the area, Alf had no room anywhere else for them due to being unable to sell them, all markets where closed, and then the day dawned. First of all a digger similar to the one that had lifted me on and off different sites came. Then Jim and his assistant arrived to value all Alf's stock. I had a feeling of some terrible disaster was about to happen, and it did. Men in their overalls and wellingtons arrived and all the young calves were unceremoniously shot in the head with a type of revolver and when they had finished I could hear further shots after which went on for about two hours. Then I heard the men talking, "that's the lot", 178 helpless animals destroyed and to be buried in a large grave. I wish I could of closed my eyes and ears and forget about that sad day. After a good scrub down with gallons of disinfectant I was then sort of redundant for a while.

Then one day I heard Alf saying "I think I am going to make this owd shed into a Farm Office, so much red tape and forms to fill up" this I was for many years. Then Alf decided to do something his mother was always going to do, write a book. This he started to do in the late 70's and then all of a

117

sudden I did not see him for many weeks. I thought I must have vexed him and then one morning he arrived. He did not look very well, quite white; he had suffered a major heart attack. He started to write again with more urgency and eventually got his first book published called "Me Dad's the Village Blacksmith". He, I know, was very proud and to show his thanks to the Royal Shrewsbury Hospital he donated all his royalties to Ward 24 Coronary Care Unit. To date something like £7,000. The cover of the Book shows his Dad with his younger brother Frank taken in 1932 with a 5/- box camera out of Paddy's market at Liverpool. The photo was taken by a girl who was on holiday in the village by the name of Howarth.

Many meetings were held in me by the cricketers on a winter's night. Warmer than their modern pavilion. By now an electric fire had been installed and of course now the tele was a must. One or two of the meetings that were held in me were with Highway Officials and Council Officers. Many were very heated and Alf used to say after they had gone, "little Hitlers". Apparently they were trying to close Alf's blacksmith demonstrations down, but Alf kept battling on and one day I remember an official with a brief case came and said he wanted more information and I heard Alf saying to him he was going to carry on because he had the support of the W.I., Women's Institute, who were going to block the main road in support of Alf's demonstrations. I remember it quite well and this certain Official went quite white and a few weeks later I heard Alf saying he was now recognised as a Tourist Attraction and I have even had Sir William Lawrence, Chairman of The Heart of England Tourist Board to see me, the Farm Office. I wonder what my other mates would think of me. I am quite a celebrity, "stuck up devil" they would say. Then in 1986 another meeting and a major decision was taken by Alf and Bernard to seperate his writing and Blacksmith demonstration from his farm pursuits and I was to be the Registered Office of Alf Strange Blacksmith and Authors Limited, The Railway Container, Brow Farm, Welsh Frankton Reg. No.

WHEELS

More promotion for me a humble Railway container has risen through the ranks from being a tree in a wood to now a Registered Office in London. Carpet now on the floor, easy chair, office desk and several chairs where will it all end. Only today I have heard words such as "we will have to have a Fax machine and a computer" and to crown all that I now attract a non domestic rate of £20.00 a year off the North Shropshire District Council. At last I am recognised as a Tourist attraction but I may not attract a rate for much longer because I believe Alf is going to put my wheel's back on after 50 years, as wheeled buildings cannot be rated. More agro from the Officials I expect but I am sure Alf will cope, he usually does.

Now my claim to fame. I am challenging any other Railway containers to beat my record:

1st – A railway container for may years.
2nd – A Cricket Pavilion for 15 years.
3rd – A farm storage shed about 3 years.
4th – A slaughter house, one night, how sad.
5th – A farm Office many years.
6th – An Author's den 15 years.
7th – A registered Office of a Limited Company.
8th – The Board Room and possibly a Fax machine and a computer to be installed for The Brow Golf Club.

AND my story is not yet complete (Phew)!

Mr Grafton Beddows

Grafton Beddows, the farmer who wrote the foreword to my first three books has sadly passed away at the age of 76. He was still a working farmer until the day he died, actually having driven a tractor on the day he passed away.

He was like most other village lads; he had played football, cricket and golf. He was a councillor and also a local lay preacher in chapel.

I went to his funeral at Prees. The church was packed with people from all walks of life and a remark by the Minister bought a wry smile to my face. He said that Grafton was a very popular man and was a member of many organisations, in fact the only one that Grafton was not a member of was the local Mothers Union!

The Grafton Beddows of this world are fast becoming a lost generation, they helped one another.

I count myself one of the lucky ones, and my life was much richer for knowing Grafton.

A fanatical Liverpool supporter

On one coach full of people from the Liverpool area was an aged gentleman whose name I do not know. On arrival he was given a cup of tea and a biscuit, he pushed the cup of tea back across the counter saying he wasn't going to drink that. When Vera asked him what was the matter with it his reply was "You don't think I am going to drink a cup of tea out of a cup that is in Everton's bloody colour." So the blue cup was emptied into a white cup and he drank it up quite happily and declared what a good cup of tea it was.

Ah well, it takes all sorts.

A feed of Fish and Chips – for two

That is what it cost me in 1950 when we were knocking down our little old smithy and building a new one. A rotten old bough of an oak tree was in our way, we wanted to raise one gable end of the smithy but alas this piece of timber was in our way. None of our gang would venture to the gable end, as we did not have the nerve to balance on one leg on the gable end and use a chainsaw at the same time.

"Send for George," said Pop Jones our bricklayer, "He will do the job for us, for the price of a feed of fish and chips for two."

This we did, and George arrived with Chris Hayward and a chainsaw. In no time at all George was standing on one leg reaching out with both arms proceeding with the chainsaw to cut the branch off. But the branch fell the wrong way and brought down the mains electric cable which of course cut off the power to all the houses and farms on the Perthy.

George and Chris disappeared to get their fish and chips leaving me to ring Manweb to get the electricity supply restored.

I explained to the girl on the telephone that the bough was very rotten and that it had fallen and bought down the electric cable.

The engineer came out quite quickly to repair the cable and remarked that he had never seen a rotten bough fall down with such a nice clean cut saw mark on it! He went on to say that if we had gone through the proper procedure, the bough could have been taken out by Manweb for free, and would have saved me the cost of fish and chips – for two!

How when we look back at the chances we took and we wish we had taken more photographs. I can still see George balancing on one leg on the end of the old gable end some 15ft from the ground.

Safety Inspectors, what were they?

A night to remember

May 8th is a date for me to remember for two reasons. The first was being the day the war with Germany finished way back in 1945. That was the night that Ellesmere Young Farmers played Houn..t Young Farmers in a challenge football match with a £1 per man for the winners. The account of that match is my second book 'Following Me Dad' was that really 55 years ago.

The second reason for me to remember May 8th is more recent, 1999 in fact. I had just finished giving an after dinner speech to the members and their wives and friends at the Brow Golf Club, when all of a sudden out of the blue I fell forward, Bang, out for the count! An ambulance was called, and I was whisked away semi-concious to The Royal Shrewsbury Hospital, Casualty department. Apparently I had low blood pressure, causing me to black out. It was a Saturday night, about 10.30pm when I arrived there and there was no 5 star treatment here amongst the drunks and drug takers and policemen breathalysing others. After a thorough examination I was taken to a ward and put into bed.

After a fairly restless night I awoke next morning to find myself in a ward that was mainly full of aged gentlemen, geriatrics we were called, what a shock that was to my system. After many more tests over the next few days, I was finally declared fit to go home, but on the Tuesday afternoon one more test was needed, Doctors wanted to monitor my heartbeat for 24 hours. Unfortunately I had to wait until a heart monitor became available which would not be until the Wednesday, I was able to get out of bed and walk around so time did go more quickly than if I had been made to stay in bed. Thursday came and I really was eager to get home but I had to wait for a Doctor or Senior Nurse to discharge me, by now it was late in the afternoon and I was really keen to get home. An elderly gentleman called me over to his bed and asked me:

"Why are you in such a hurry to get home today Alf? Why don't you stay here and get some rest while you can" he added.

I replied "I have got plenty to do at home."

He then said "You want to stay until tomorrow afternoon."

"Why?" I said, "What happens then?"

"Well" he said "We always have fish and chips for dinner on Fridays."

Just another ray of sunshine in another day of my life a treat for him, fish and chips on a Friday, that remark really puts life into true perspective. Not much to look forward to in our modern society, when going out for a meal quite regularly is the modern trend. Every time we have fish and chips I wonder what happened to him, I hope he is at home still enjoying fish and chips, and not only on a Friday.

Life can be so cruel

Life can be so very cruel.

In 1975 we decided to buy out a local riding school which was owned and managed by Major Halstead on condition that he came to manage it for me for twelve months to get it going in its new quarters. There were about ten ponies complete with their saddles and bridles etc. There was also a good cross section of customers and private schools, enough to keep the Major busy through the week and with the help of casual labour at a weekend and I was able to shoe my own ponies also we had our own grazing and hay.

Things went along very smoothly for a while until one morning Major Halstead announced he was going back into the Army, the lure of the Middle East had proved too much for him having spent a lot of time abroad. We had only a short time to find a replacement for him. His replacement was a young lady named Ann Raybould, her father was Vicar of St Martins.

The Riding School was building up trade and with the help of a country cottage for riding holidays it was not long before we were wanting another full time girl. Out of the blue came a letter from a lass in London who used to come on holidays to her Granny's in Gobowen a village near-by she was wondering if there were any jobs going at The Forge Riding School, her name was Susan Davies.

Susan was contacted and was able to start work for us fairly quickly, but as usual things in business only run smoothly for a while. Ann decided she wanted to leave to go and work elsewhere, so we were back to square one. Susan was fully able to take over the role of Head Girl, and the Riding School with the help of two local girls, Sharon Harrocks and Joy Barclay continued to flourish. Susan was by now living in our 'Granny' flat and she always used to say that when she married it would be to a working farmer, as she wanted to be involved herself with the sheep and cattle, a working wife herself, having been a town girl.

By now having reached the age of 55 myself and with a 100 acre farm to run and also a full time farrier, and my own two children not wanting to farm or blacksmith, the decision was made to sell the Riding School as a going concern with its house and buildings. It was soon sold to a lady who had been a secretary for a large company, and had informed me soon after that she had dealt with as many millions of pounds as I had hundreds in my lifetime.

Susan by now had left to go to work at a pony trekking centre, and it was not long before the Riding School was up for sale. There is lot of difference in dealing in millions of pounds and running a Riding School in the middle of a rural area, a small business requires the personal touch, and also one has to be a little bit humble at certain times.

Susan eventually found her working farmer and the marriage took place at Pontfadog Church with a horse drawn carriage to take her to church and the reception was held at The Glyn Valley Hotel. It was a lovely country wedding, but it was one of the coldest days I can ever remember, I had only just come out of hospital after a major heart attack. Susan and Andrew farmed successfully for many years and along came two children, Elisabeth and David.

Susan's father had retired from his job, working on the maintenance of aircraft at Heathrow Airport. He and his wife Joan came to live in the area. Then a cruel fate arose in the family, Andrew, Susan's husband had a terminal illness and within a couple of years she lost her father to whom she was very close and her husband Andrew died at the tender age of 40, and her mother also suffered a stroke. What a burden to bear in a couple of years, for one so young to have to face.

Ann Raybould lost her husband Jeff Davies, who died at the early age of 37, and also Major Halstead had died. So in a short space of time four husbands whom I had known very well succumbed to one illness or another.

125

Susan today is still farming, and with the help of a friend takes care of about 750 sheep, (numbers rising as we write due to the lambing season!!), she also runs boarding kennels, a cattery, a livery stable, as well as having about 12 horses and 11 dogs of her own, so she is well and truly a country girl now.

At Andrew's funeral a poem was read by Arwyn Jones, with which I would like to end this chapter. This all happened in a few short years.

> I thank thee God that I have lived,
> In this great world and known its many joys;
> The songs of birds, the strong sweet smell of hay
> And cooling breezes in the secret dusk.
> The flaming sunsets at the close of day,
> Hills, and the lonely, heather covered moors,
> Music at night and moonlight on the sea,
> The beat of waves upon the rocky shore
> And wild white spray, flung high in ecstasy;
> The faithful eyes of dogs, and treasured books.
> The love of kin and fellowship of friends,
> And all that makes life dear and beautiful.
> I thank thee too, that there has come to me
> A little sorrow and sometimes defeat,
> A little heartache and the loneliness
> That comes with parting and the word 'Good-bye'
> Dawn breaking after weary hours of pain
> When I discovered that night's gloom must yield
> And morning light break through to me again,
> Because of these and other blessings poured
> Unasked upon my wondering head.
> Because I know that there is yet to come
> An even richer and more glorious life,
> And most of all, because thine only Son
> Once sacrificed life's loveliness for me—
> I thank thee God, that I have lived.
>
> *Elizabeth Craven.*

To rescue a chicken or save a life

Another true story that happened was the time an aged gentleman came into the ward. He apparently had had pains in his chest the week before, caused by angina. After a few days he was allowed home. He was preparing dinner at his home for his nephew and his wife who were coming to visit him. Halfway through preparing the meal he had more pains in his chest, another attack of angina and having been told that if he had any more attacks he was to telephone for an ambulance straight away, this he did.

The ambulance arrived, and in his haste to get to the hospital he forgot to switch off the electric oven which was cooking his chicken for dinner. Five miles down the road on the way to the Royal Shrewsbury Hospital he requested that the ambulance men stop and turn around and go back to his cottage so that he could nip in and turn the cooker off. I can only guess what remarks the driver would have made.

Which was more important, getting a patient to hospital or rescuing a burnt chicken out of the oven.

To the best of my knowledge, the gentleman in question is still alive and well.

A Dog's life

When I bought the little terrier bitch from a Mrs Jennings of Cheswardine little did I think what a part she was to play in my future life. I bought her in about 1968 and the obvious name for her was 'Jenny.' She always seemed to be with me, and I am sure if she could have talked, she would have done. Two years after my first spell in hospital 1980 I was away for about 14 days and when I arrived home she would not have anything to do with me, like as if I had gone away without telling her. But after a few days she was back to normal and hardly left my side.

I would say to her do a twirl if you want to go for a walk, this she would do on her hind legs just like a ballerina. Also she could be the far end of our big back lawn and I would shout to her "are you coming for a walk?" she would come as fast as her little legs would carry her, and when she got about a yard away from me she would take one almighty leap into my arms almost knocking me over. As I got to feel better our walks would be getting longer up to 5 miles or more. For the last mile or so she would begin to tire and start to fall behind I used to say to her "Come on, get on to my shoulders" I would bend down and she would climb up on to my shoulders. Her back and front legs would be wrapped around my neck and we continue with the rest of our journey home.

Many was the time in the early days after my illness that I did not feel like going, but she used to make me get up out of my armchair, even if it were raining or snowing. And as we all know now that exercise is the finest cure for any heart problems. So I can recommend to any one with heart problems – buy a dog.

Jenny lived to the ripe old age of 18 and sadly passed away

one Saturday morning leaving a gap in my life which I can not describe. She is laid to rest at the bottom of our big lawn, along with my other two terriers, Bogey and Trixie. Rest in Peace, all three of you.

The photo is of Jenny sitting on my shoulders when she was getting a bit tired. It was taken at the bottom of Norman, Freda, Mike and Jill's garden overlooking the bottom road fields that we would walk over for many hours. My first terrier whose name was Bogey is the singing dog mentioned in my first book 'Me Dad's the Village Blacksmith'

A Domineering Woman in the party

Booked in for a visit to my smithy was a group of ladies who were arriving at about 6 p.m. Tea coffee and biscuits had been ordered for about 7.15pm. then they were going on a mystery trip around the area, they did not require an evening meal as they were hoping to be home for about 9 o'clock.

The trip for them was being paid for by the local Round Table, but alas when they arrived one lady in the group demanded a cup of tea before my demonstration, in fact she sat down in the tea-room. She also managed by this time to persuade two other ladies to join in her demand for a cup of tea.

No amount of persuading by their organiser or me to join the rest of the party in the smithy was going to change her mind. I told her that once my demonstration started the door would be bolted and no one would be allowed in. That still did not change her mind, she wanted her cup of tea. To try and explain to her that the water in the tea-room would not yet be boiled made no difference to her.

So without further ado I went into my smithy were about 40 or so other ladies were sitting on the chapel pews waiting for me to begin.

"She is a very awkward type of person," they all said.

My demonstrations are not only educational but often humorous as well and it was not long before the ladies were all laughing and having a good time. By this time the awkward woman had decided that she wanted to come in and join in the fun, but no way would she be allowed in as the doors were well and truly bolted, no amount of knocking was any use. She eventually went away and sat on the bus for an hour or so, and when the demonstration was over and tea was being served she decided that she did not want her cup of tea then.

I felt quite sorry for the Round Table lads, but we all agreed that the woman had been taught a lesson and if we had not stood up to her she could have ruined the night for the rest of the party.

Deaf People at the back of the room

One of the places I used to regularly visit to give a chat to had two partly deaf old gentlemen who always sit at the back of the room. I used to try and get them to sit nearer the front, but all to no avail. But the point was they could not hear my stories. I would be telling my stories when one old lad would say to the other "What did he say?" then the other one would be trying to repeat what I had just said. This was always very upsetting to the rest of the audience who would often turn around and tell them to be quiet.

During one of my visits they were making more noise than usual, when all of a sudden the organiser, who was a regular church going person shouted to them to be quiet and the went on to say "I will part you pair of buggers in a minute!"

His remark was totally out of character, as I myself had never heard him swear before. Sadly all three of them have gone to pastures new, just another little story in the life of a blacksmith.

Visiting cricket teams think they are playing at Lords when they see Frankton Cricket Club's new weather vane. It was made by Jack and Alf Strange for the 'Millennium.' It will eventually grace their new pavilion. Looking on are the founder members of the club.

Left to Right: Alf Strange, Peter Done, Jack Haynes, Col. Kynaston, Robert Mainwaring (president), Bill Strange and Jack Strange.

A wet Saturday morning in April 1995

We awoke on that Saturday morning to a very wet scene, staying with us for a few days were our Canadian cousins, Ruth and Elsie and Ruth's daughter, Elizabeth.

Where to go and what to find them to do on such a wet morning was going to be a problem. So, first of all, we went up to our little Congregational Chapel where their Dad and Grandmother were christened and also worshipped there. Ruth played the organ beautifully to the tune of one of her Dads favourite hymns, – 'Son of My Soul.' My brother Jack and I joined in, it was a very emotional for a few moments, with no shortage of tears.

Then racking my brain what to do next, when the thought suddenly came to me. I had recently found out where my cousin's and my Grandmother was born, it was at a farmhouse between Cockshutt and Burlton. So without further ado we loaded up the car and away we went, not knowing what sort of welcome, if any, we would get from the owner of the house.

Knocking on the door of the farmhouse, a gentleman opened it. I explained briefly who I was and apologised for calling out of the blue with three Canadian ladies and explained who they were.

All my fears went in the first few moments, we could not have received a warmer welcome if we had been Royalty.

"Come in and feel free to wander anywhere you wish," he said, and a cup of coffee appeared in no time at all. I myself was emotionally touched as remember it was my Granny as well as the girls, who had lived there – to stand in the same kitchen where their granny lived some years ago, the tears and the silence said it all. A memory that will last forever.

The gentleman who had made us so welcome was a Mr Evans, and the farm was called Wackly Lodge, Nr Cockshutt and Burlton. After many years of meeting Americans and Canadians I find them to be a very emotional type. They love our history, as I don't think they have history back home like we do over here.

Alf telling his Canadian cousins one of his tales.

The Salters of Stanham

(Mrs Colleen Cubberly who was a maid for the Salter family during the last war writes the following chapter.)

My maiden name was Colleen Jones. I lived in the village of Tetchill, which is halfway between Ellesmere and Frankton where my story starts.

With my sister Ivy, on a Sunday afternoon, we would set off to Frankton Congregational Chapel while Dad had his 'Sunday Snooze.' Frankton Lane was a typical English Lane; it wound its way shaded by Oak trees. Halfway up we came to a steep hill known as 'Tabny Gwynt.' At the bottom of Tabny Gwynt on the left hand side was a firtree wood, this we always called Salters Wood. As you climbed the steep hill there were pale primroses in the spring with violets and young green ferns, and when you reached the top there was a lovely bluebell wood.

Now we came to the big gates of Brynallt. There was a cottage at the side where Mr Powell lived with his wife and two daughters. I can only remember Grace, she was very delicate. We would carry on up the lane, which bordered Brynallt; Ivy and I never loitered here for it always seemed gloomy. As we came to Frankton Chapel the 'Strange Boys' would be waiting with other pals. While we stood chatting by the wall waiting for Mr Carsley to open up, along would pass Miss May Salter who always gave us a smile and a nod on her way to Church Sunday school. Miss Howie Salter was also a Sunday school teacher.

Before we continue any further I must tell of a simple village girl – Mary Morris, who was employed at Brynallt as a maid.

In the 'big houses' around the district lunch was mid-day afternoon tea was at 4 o'clock, and dinner was at 7 o'clock.

After dinner the family retired to the drawing room, while the servants washed the dishes and set out the breakfast things ready for the morning, they could never relax in the servant's hall.

One night the drawing room bell rang and Mary went to answer it, 'Oh Mary, will you put some coal on the fire.'

Mary with four nods of her head answered:

"What with one, two, three, four of you here and none of you can put a bit of coal on the fire."

I never did find out what happened next.

In July 1939 I was fourteen, finished school and had one week at home, when Mother on her weekly shopping trip to Ellesmere had met Miss Salter who said she was looking for a maid. An interview was arranged a few days later. Now I had often passed Stanham but had no idea who lived there, but I was about to find out.

Mother and I passed through a huge green wooden gate, followed the curved path flanked with trees and on to the big house. Miss Ada who I had never met opened the door; she led us in to the Drawing Room. It was lovely, with a white marble fireplace with Grecian figures down the side and four big windows overlooking the gardens.

Miss Salter sat in her chair and Miss Ada stood by her, it was arranged that I start work the following week, on one month's trial at 7s 6d per week, and my keep, one half day off a week (Thursday) and every other Sunday afternoon. Cook had Saturday and the other Sunday.

The following week we went shopping for my uniform. In the morning I was to wear a pale blue dress with a white cap and apron and black lisle stockings, (oh horror). I had never worn anything other than ankle socks. When I see girls of today with thick black stockings, they look so fashionable, but I hated mine.

Afternoons, I was to change into a black dress with a white collar and cuff, head cap and small apron. I didn't have a black dress so Miss Ada gave me one, it was alpaca. Looking through some things last year I still have that dress, it won't fit me now though!!

Perhaps I should describe Stantham as I saw it. On the left of the Hall was the drawing room, and on the right the dining room. At the far end of the hall was a wide curved staircase with a small morning room to the right. Upstairs Mrs Salter's was the first room on your left, then came the guest room which was huge. You could easily have put four four-poster beds in it. At the end of the landing was an alcove with a treadle sewing machine. Now coming back along the landing were Miss May, Howie and Ada's room's which all faced south.

There were two bathrooms and the stairs led to the top floor which had seven rooms, but only cook and I used this part.

In some of the rooms were cases belonging to the Salters who travelled quite a bit, by the labels on the trunks. I almost forgot Mary's room (Mrs Webster) which was at the bottom of our staircase.

Now to describe the Salters. Mrs Salter was a tall lady, her hairstyle was the same as when she was first married. She always wore a black skirt of ankle length and a grey silk blouse.

Mary was a big person, with mid brown hair caught at the nape of the neck. She was a 'Top Dog' in the nursing for Shropshire, as was Howie but not quite so important. Miss Howie was a little mouse like person, with short blonde hair and blue eyes. I think she found it hard to make decisions, her favourite saying was "oh – oh dear." Ada was a slim 5ft 6ins person, with long hair which she wore plaited and then like earphones, her eyes were blue and she wore glasses. I think she would have made a good solicitor, when she looked at you she weighed you up, as did Hugh Salter when he was a little boy. Mary had long light brown hair which she wore plaited across the back of her head, when she joined the RAF she had it cut. She had blue eyes and a smashing figure also a good pair of legs; she could adapt to anything and was a real character.

After I had been at Stanham a month I was taken on permanent and my wages were 10 shillings a week.

September 3rd war was declared, we had shutters made for the big windows, and Clawley the gardener would lift them in to position every night before he went home. The cellar, which reached the full length under the house, was made into an Air raid Shelter with blankets and everything we might need in an emergency.

Although war was declared we tried to carry on as normal life in the big houses and most weeks someone had a tennis party. When one was held at Stanham, I had learned how to make bitesized tomato sandwiches. You put a tomato in to a cup and then pour boiling water on it, when the skin splits you take it out and peel the skin off, mash it with some salt and pepper cut some thin bread and butter and there you are.

Tea was always served in the drawing room and Mrs. Salter sat at a small table with a brass kettle and a silver teapot and poured the tea. The tennis court at Stanham was in front of the house so after I had washed up I would creep on to the landing to watch. Mary was the only one who played and her tennis dress had been specially made for her. She was a good player and towards the end she would do a sort of a grand slam, she would hit the ball and twirl at the same time. Her dress with its full circular skirt would lift like an umbrella showing her close fitting pants. It was brilliant. It did make Dr Rogers eyes twinkle!

The Salters of America

The next few pages tell the story of the Salters of America and Ellesmere and Welsh Frankton. I have decided not to alter the manuscript at all but to leave it as it was written by Bert Lockwood Salter from America. Bert has given me permission to use it as I wish.

I am sure it will revive a lot of memories for the people of Welsh Frankton and the Ellesmere area. My Thanks to Bert for his permission.

Abby Farr Salter was the eleventh and last child of James and Mary Salter. In this case the last shall be first for two main reasons, first there is more useful information on her, including a number of letters and photos than on most of her siblings. Second she had a key part in perpetuating the James Salter line in England, as her brother Charles did in the U.S.A. Her story moreover is unusually interesting.

Abby (the spelling appears as such in the earliest Salter family records and censuses) was born on February 11th 1869, in her parents home at 1022 Lafayette Avenue in Brooklyn New York. She apparently was named after an elderly neighbour Abbie Farr, who lived just a few houses away at that time. She probably did not know her namesake and may have rebelled against her middle name as a child. A census record indicated that as early as 1880 when she was 11 years old she was using Anne as a middle name. Later documents including those with her own signature gave her name as Annie Anne.

Abbie grew up in the Lafayette homestead with brothers and sisters considerably older than she. The gap between her and the next oldest sibling, Emma was 6 years. (This is because the tenth child in the Salter family, Joseph Wright

Salter died before Abbie was born. She may have known her oldest siblings only distantly. Her sister Mary Jane for example married at 22 and moved to Texas with her husband Charles Cooper, when Abbie was only 5 years old. At the same time her brother Charles was 17 and about to embark on his first voyage as a merchant seaman. The census records reveal that in 1880, by the time she was 11, the only children of James and Mary Salter permanently residing at home were her four older unmarried sisters – Mary Louisa (30) Charlotte (24) Fannie (19) and Emma (17).

Without a brother or sister close to her age Abbie must have looked for friends in the neighbourhood to play with. One such friend probably was Jennie Lockwood, the daughter of Frederick Ebbets Lockwood and Mary Titus who was only one month older than Abbie and who lived a few houses away at 1039 Lafayette Avenue, Jennie and Abbie grew up knowing each other and probably attended the same schools throughout their childhood. In 1889 when they were 20 Abbie and Jennie became sisters-in-law as Jennie was married to Abbie's widowed brother Charles.

Of course, Abbie would have developed many other friendships in her youth. Chief among these in terms of lasting relationships were members of the John Horton family. The tie to the Hortons was twofold. In October 1881 when Abbie was 12, her oldest sister Maria Louisa married John Horton, whose first wife had died. Two years later John Horton's eldest daughter, Harriet married Abbie's brother, Charles. It is not likely that in the next few years Abbie was very close to Harriett Horton who was 9 years older than she. In any case, Harriett died in 1888, in her fifth year of marriage. On the other hand Abbie did develop a life long friendship with Harriets younger sister, Fannie.

Marriage came to Abbie on June 7th 1893. Introducing another unusual twist to her family relationships, she married her English cousin, Kiffin George Salter, who had met Abbie when he was in America on business. They were married at her parents' home (then located at 774 Greene Avenue in Brooklyn) by the Rev. H. Richard Harris. Her parents signed the marriage certificate as witnesses. 24, then left America permanently to commence married life with her 50-year old husband on the Salter estate, Brynallt, near Welsh Frankton in Shropshire, England. And thus a new chapter in her life opened up.

In the course of the next 10 years Abbie gave birth to six children at Brynallt. Their names and birthdates are as follows:

Mary Edwa (May 15 1894)
Emma Harward (November 12 1895)
Ada Langford (May 12 1897)
Lillian Webster (August 3 1898)
Jackson George Kyffin (Aug 7 1901)
Mary Whilton (December 8 1904)

As previously indicated the middle names derived from families connected with the English Salters reflecting Kyffin George's strong interest in his ancestry.

Clearly family mattered a great deal to Abbie as well. Numerous pictures of her family mostly of her children have survived on glass negatives that she produced in a darkroom set in the basement at Brynallt, made at the end of the last century and the first part of this, these amateurish photo's presumably were intended strictly for viewing at home. Relatives in America received numerous professionally made portraits of her children and herself.

Surviving correspondence provides interesting glimpses into Abbie's life and her devotion to her family. A letter from Abbie's mother Mary Salter to Abbie's sister-in-law Jennie dated 10 June 1899 is worth quoting in part.

My Dear Jennie,
In my last letter to Abbie about a month ago I told of the arrival of your little daughter. I got her answer about 3 days ago and she desires her love to you and Charlie and congratulations to you on the birth of your little daughter, saying it will be a great comfort to jennie as her 4 little comforts are to her!! Abbie has had a cake for little May with

5 candles on it so you see she is keeping up with the American fashion and a good one I think . . .

Living in England did not entirely separate Abbie from her American friends and relations. As Abbie's daughter Mary Webster (hereafter referred to as MWW) explained in a letter to your historian-editor, Fannie Horton married and moved to England at some point when MWW was a child, dated September 1982 it says in part:

> Incidentally Mother had a great friend with whom she grew up in the U.S.A. who came to live in Woking, Surrey; Tiny Frech nee Horton. Mother always said she was "not quite" a relation but we called her Aunt Tiny. (Actually she was as tall as Mother, about 5´9˝ or 5´10˝). Tiny used to stay often with us at Brynallt. Tiny and Alfred Frech had one daughter, Kathleen, six months older than me. Apparently Aunt Tiny's mother pierced her and Mother's ears – with a needle and cork! So Aunt Tiny insisted that Kathleen and I should go through the same ceremony together – though professionally. Kathleen fainted but I didn't!!

What Mary didn't realise was that this "great friend" of her Mother's was actually Fannie Horton, the sister of Abbie's deceased sister-in-law Harriett.

Abbie's life at Brynallt was altered radically on October 26 1914 when her husband died. Now at the age of 42 she was solely responsible for maintaining Brynallt and raising her family. According to MWW she was very strict with the children, as her husband had been.

Indeed, it cannot have been an easy life for Abbie despite the help of several servants. During World War I or the Great War as it was called, Shropshire's male population had its fair share of casualties. Perhaps the most famous such casualty was the "war poet" – anti-war poet is more the appropriate tag – Wilfred Owen full name Wilfred Edward Owen Salter Owen, whose family according to MWW were often guests of the Salters. The thinned ranks of eligible young men may account in part for the fact that of Abbie's five daughters only the youngest, Mary married.

Abbie continued to reside at Brynallt until her son Jack married in 1935 at which time she yielded the estate to him and moved with her unmarried daughters into a smaller but still comfortably sized house in Ellesmere that her husband had provided for her to use. A year later her only married daughter was widowed herself and returned to live with her Mother and sisters.

The house in Ellesmere was called originally "The Avenue" and then "Stanham" According to MWW, Abbie changed the name after a gale blew down most of the trees that created "the avenue" leading to the house. The new name which meant "a walled garden" reflected the fact that the property was surrounded by a wall 12ft high.

Several letters that Abbie wrote to her relatives in America chronicle some of the important events in her life. Excerpts from these letters follow.

(Christmas 1936) Stanham, Ellesmere, Salop, England.

Dear Arthur,

It is such a long time since hearing from you that I fear you have forgotten your old Aunt Abbie . . . We like our new home, but I miss my son [Jack] & the lovely view of old home.

Did you know a baby boy [Hugh] has arrived to give them a Merry Christmas . . .

With kind love to you and all the family,
Your affect.
Aunt Abbie Salter.

(June 26 1938) Stanham, Ellesmere, Shropshire, England.

My Dear Niece (Addye)

A few days ago I received the notice of your marriage and now write to wish you and your husband every happiness in your life. It is a long time since hearing anything of my brother Charlie's family; Arthur used to write occasionally but has not done so for many years, although I have written several times. You will see that I am no longer living at Brynallt. My daughters and I came here about three years ago when my son Jackson was married. He is now living at

143

the old home with a very nice wife and a little son (Hugh) 20 months old. Needless to say he is very dear to us all. I am quite an old person being 69, and unfortunately very deaf, but can hear with an electric ear phone, but like most Salters have good health.

December 2nd 1940

My Dear Nephew (Arthur)

It seems impossible that Christmas is so near, how different it all is now, but people in this favoured spot try to carry on as much as possible. The blackout makes the days too short to do much. The planes fly over here on their way to Liverpool where they have done much damage. We do not hear details till later on. Our little town of about 1000 has 700 soldiers billeted here with their officers, so with all the refugees staying with friends the place is quite full.

How thankful we should be (and are) to be where we are. We were in Chester last week and had an air raid warning, but it passed over. Since then we hear that the lovely Cathedral has been bombed. What spite they have on the churches – no military gain at all, just bent on destruction of life and property. When in Chester I bought the only sleigh for my grandsons Christmas.

(April 17, 1941) Stanham, Ellesmere Salop, England

My dear Nephew (Robert)

Your letter received a few days ago was a great surprise and pleasure coming from such an unexpected quarter, as I seldom hear from my sisters now, so many ships being lost. The battle of the Atlantic is a terrible thing, and the news from Europe is very grave. Up to the present the neighbourhood has been free from bombs, but being in the direct "lane" they call it, enemy planes often pass over on their way to Liverpool etc., where there has been heavy bombing again this week.

When the bombers come over we get warnings and then May and Mary have to report for duty. We are told not to use our iron rations (tinned food) to keep them in case of an invasion. We have an officer billeted here, a French gentleman came over with a part of the Army from Dunkirk,

144

the remaining being prisoners in Germany. Although I am the youngest of the family I am 72 so cannot expect to carry on as usual. Jack has two sons, Hugh 4½ and Richard 2½. Needless to say they are very dear to me. They are having tea with me tomorrow. Any chocolate I get I keep for them.

Pansy wrote telling me about her husband (Arthur's) death, it seems he wrote to me a week before but unfortunately I did not get his letter. It is almost impossible to buy any tin goods, knits etc. stockings and underwear shops almost sold out. Will germans always be spoken of as "The Enemy"?

Fortunately, Abbie lived to witness the tide turn in the war in Europe. She died at the age of 75 on July 5th 1944 and was buried in the family plot in the graveyard of St. Andrews Church in Welsh Frankton.

A night out speaking to Oswestry Rotarians.
Left to Right: Bob Humphreys, Alf Strange, Brian Case and John Bilsley.

A visit from the Children of Chernobyl

In the last few years we have had to our Farm Museum and Blacksmith Demonstration two parties of children from the Chernobyl area of Russia. One party came in 1993 and the other came in 1997. The majority of the children had been affected by the nuclear fall out which meant that some of the children would not reach adulthood.

When we had the first group of children to visit us, it was very emotional for a while. Here was a bunch of children with a limited life span doing exactly what our English Children would do. Sitting on my old vintage tractors, blowing the fire up with the old bellows, playing football in the paddock, laughing and singing as if they hadn't got a care in the world.

They were here for about 3 hours, then we had a picnic on the lawn after which they left to go on to Telford to go ice-skating and ten-pin bowling, followed by tea at McDonalds.

One little incident I remember was they had been travelling for 3 days by train across Russia to get here, when on arrival one of the treats the organisers had in store for them was a train ride at Llangollen!. Still the thought was there.

As they got on the coach to go one thought how would I have reacted, children's lives at risk to satisfy man's greed.

The second party of Chernobyl children came in 1997. They were no different to the first party, maybe a little younger but still very well behaved. They asked many questions through an interpreter, who as I recall was a very attractive blonde girl about 27 years old, needless to say we got on very well!! No problems arose in our conversations.

I felt very humble and considered it an honour to have been involved in bringing a little bit of happiness to the children who had suffered so much in their very short lives.

Blighted Lives – These children from Chernobyl, visiting the Smithy in 1997 may never reach adulthood – due to man's greed.

A little bit of advice

If I may I would like to say a few words to the so-called bureaucrats of our society. As someone who has worked for 61 years, 55 of them for myself as a small businessman. My life would have been a whole lot easier if when one had had a good idea it would have not been shot down, leaving me to appeal. Appeals cost money. Small businesses, in my opinion, are the backbone of this wonderful country of ours, and if 'THEY' could only remember when they adjust our Council Tax today, and invariably it goes up, it adds extra cost to the job tomorrow.

Remember a little business needs a vehicle and a telephone and it is not always a 9 to 5 job. What I would like to see is someone to come out and discuss your plans with you, not send you forms which require the assistance of a solicitor to fill them in. A young person can arrive with a briefcase and in it he or she thinks they have all the answers.

When you have been in business for a good length of time, one can say you have been to University, 'The University of Life' and what you have learnt in that time cannot be found in any books. A bunch of letters after your name are not much use if you have not got any common sense. The best degree you can get is the one which only comes with experience.

One morning one of the new breed of officials whom I would be seeing a lot of over the next few years arrived. As usual he was about an hour late, and in fact I pointed that out to him. I remember thinking how young he was to hold down such a job. I introduced myself as Alf, as I prefer this to Mr Strange, and I enquired what his Christian name was. His reply really shook me, he informed me that he wished to be call Mr . . . . whatever his name was. Needless to say we got on like a house on fire, enough said, end of story!

The Dolls Houses find a new home

I received a telephone call from a Mr Molyneux of Norbury asking me if I could go and see a Mr Bill Ankers his neighbour who used to work on the Chomondley Estate not far from Whitchurch. Now this Bill Ankers had a hobby and that hobby was making model dolls' houses, castles, palaces and pubs etc. He would make them out of any old bits of wood or scrap metal he could find. He had been making them for about 40 years or so and I reckon when he finished he had about 80 to 100 or so in his collection. It turned out that Mr Ankers was moving house, I think actually it was an old people's home and I was asked if I would like some of them to go into my museum.

I set off to go and see them and when I arrived I couldn't believe it they were lovely. They were all set out in a village like setting, little streets with pubs and a post office in. There were castles with toy cannons and little castle cottages. There were foreign temples and Royal palaces; there was even a model of Coronation Street along with the Rovers Return.

I decided to try and rescue some of them, I went along with my brother Jack and a friend of ours from Welshampton, Mr Frank Bailey. It took us about 10 days to do what we had to do, as unfortunately as we tried to move them many of them fell apart. I think we managed to save about 25 to 30 of them, but it poured with rain every day we were there. We left about 30 or so there which were going to be a bit harder to move as they were the worse for wear through being outside, we left these there and went home to try and make a type of stretcher on which to carry them to the roadside and then on to our truck.

We went back about a week later but sadly someone had been in the garden smashed them all up, put them in a corner and burnt them – a priceless collection spoilt. I wonder if the person who did this tragic deed realised that in a few short hours they had destroyed a lifetime's work.

The sad end to this story is that Mr Ankers passed away about a fortnight or so after moving to his new home, probably from a broken heart, but I am glad to have rescued a few of them and they remain together in my museum. They look lovely now and with a new coat of paint and a bit of a tidy up are quite an attr   ·ion especially for the young ones.

Some of the Model Houses – many were lost.

Oh be thankful, count your blessings oh be grateful

(written by my brother Bill)

Please God forgive me when I whine, for I am blessed indeed
the world is mine.

Today upon a bus I saw a lovely maid with golden hair,
She looked so gay with envy I wished I was as fair,
When suddenly she rose to leave, I saw her hobble down the
    aisle,
She had one foot and one crutch, but as she passed a smile.
Please God forgive me when I whine I have two feet I am
    blessed indeed, the world is mine.

Later I stopped to buy a paper the lad who sold them had
    such charm,
I talked to him, he said to me "It's nice to talk to folk like
    you, you see I'm blind."
Please God forgive me when I whine, I am blessed indeed I
    have two eyes the world is mine.

With feet to take me I'd go, with eyes to watch the sunset
    glow,
With ears to hear the song of birds, with a nose to smell the
    scent of flowers and herbs,
With hands to reach for the skies above, and with lips to kiss
    the ones I love, Thank-you God.
Forgive me when I whine, I am blessed indeed, 'The world is
    mine'

My elder brother Bill and Win his wife. Sadly Bill passed away on November 6th, 1999. Luckily I had got Bill to read my 4th book before it went to print. I asked him what he thought of it. His reply was "It's all right." Those remarks coming from an elder brother are real praise indeed.

Don't give up

Don't give up, you may be tempted to, but don't give up
When you have lost the desire to try,
And you've misplaced your hopeful dreams,
dare to believe again in the impossible,
Catch a ray of sunshine, and hold on tightly,
The one who holds your hand,
Will never let you go.

(This piece of verse was found in brother Bill's wallet after he passed away – it was marked for Alf.)

Farewell Bernard

Sadly today, November 23rd was the day of the funeral of Bernard Hallett the accountant from Ellesmere.

We first met on pushbikes in the year of 1948 at his office in Trimpley Hall Ellesmere some 52 years ago.

I said a few words at his funeral, he was not only my accountant, – he was a friend as well and he assisted me in compiling my books.

Farewell Bernard.

Excitement at Babbinswood

Doug Gough, a friend of mine for many years, lives at Babbinswood near Whittingham. He is a first class swimming instructor, a sergeant major in the army during the 1939-45 war, he is chairman of the Royal Artillery Association and one would say he is willing to help out at any function in the area. He is also a life saving instructor and takes his two imitation demonstration dolls, called mannequins, to various organisations to instruct them in the art of life saving – the kiss of life etc.

One day he was taking his 'dummies' to Criftins, a village just a few miles away to demonstrate his skills. His car boot was full of other things and he was having great difficulty in getting the boot lid down as either a leg or an arm or a head kept popping out of his boot. After some difficulty he managed to get the dummies safely in and popped back into the house to say goodbye to his wife Olive.

Suddenly all hell was let loose, two police cars with sirens blaring pulled up outside his house, policemen with truncheons were everywhere. Apparently someone had been going past in a car, saw Doug struggling to get the boot lid down and had telephoned the police to say a man was putting a body into the boot of a car. Doug protested and was having a laugh. On opening the boot lid, out shot the dummies body.

Another case sorted in a matter of minutes and a good laugh was had by all concerned – Shades of Del Boy.

The Sequel – Sixty Years On

In our village of Welsh Frankton in the early 1930s three boys were born within six months of one another, within a hundred yards of one another. They went to Welsh Frankton Church of England school together and in one school photograph the three sit crossed legged in the front row side by side. Their names were Lewis Edwards, Ron Jones and Maurice Jones.

They went through their school days together and when they left school used to go to the pictures in Oswestry together. Some nights they would play billiards or snooker together. One could almost bet that where one was the other two were not far away. Lewis Edwards did not marry but ran a haulage and coal business in the village of Welsh Frankton. Eventually ill health forced early retirement to Shrewsbury to live with his sister Nesta for many years, eventually passing away at the early age of sixth-one.

Ron left Welsh Frankton to go to work for the Crosville bus company in Chester as a carpenter. After a while he came back to Welsh Frankton to take over his father's trailer building business, and also his undertaker's business. He buried Lewis one of his best mates. Little did we think that in a very short time Ron himself would pass away quite suddenly of a heart attack at work one morning only a few months after Lew.

Maurice joined the Airforce and travelled the world over. He eventually married and went to work and live in Wrenbury a village some thirty miles away. Thirty odd years later he died in a tragic car accident, a few months after Ron, his sister Janet sang his favourite hymn at his funeral, a request he had made some years previous.

So here you have three lads born within a few months of

one another, within a few yards of one another, went their various ways in life and in their sixties all died within a few months of one another. They are all laid to rest in Welsh Frankton churchyard within a few yards of one another.

(The photograph showing these three lads is in my second book – "Following me Dad")

A *fast stretch of road*

As I have mentioned many times the road on which we live is a very fast stre.   of road. Traffic comes over the top of the Brow at excessive speed past our place it would be impossible for some of them to stop should there happen to be a veheicle stationary or broke down. And I dread to think what could happen should a child be on the road.

I once said to one of the Highways Officials that I was concerned for the safety of my six grandchildren whom all live close by. His reply was, "Well there is a simple answer to that you should move!!"

After 75 years that was the thinking of the Highway Policy. No need for many letters after your name to make remarks like that.

A Sad Day at Cloy Hall

Reminiscing through the pages of my first book the other day when it suddenly struck me that an incident, which happened some 52 years ago, repeated itself. On my 65th birthday I bought myself a pony and gig, and also a vintage Morris 8 Tourer 1935. Having worked with horses all my life, I decided it was time to have a little bit of pleasure, but life doesn't always work out as you expect it to.

We had started to do blacksmith demonstrations in our old reconstructed village smithy and life became quite hectic, more and more coaches were arriving from all over the country bringing people to see me. This was fine but it meant that I had less time for a ride in the pony and gig, so I lent my pony called 'Bagle' to the granddaughter of Mr. Fred Machin from Cloy Hall. She was a lass of about 17 years old named Sarah, and she had a younger sister called Helen. Six months was the agreed time for Bagle to stay with them on their farm. I knew that she would be very well looked after and also that she would be ridden regularly which is what she needed.

Well the six months ran into 12 months and I was still no better fixed to have her back: I was still kept very busy in my smithy. Then one morning out of the blue Fred came into our farmyard, took out his cheque book from his pocket and said to me "I have come to buy Bagle off you, there is no way my granddaughter will let you have her back."

I thought it was more important for Sarah to have her than me, so I told Fred to keep her for another six months.

"No" said Fred, "I want to buy her now, put your price on her."

This I did. I sold Bagle to Fred for the same price as I paid for her a few years earlier.

One morning some eighteen months later, Fred rang me

and I could tell from his voice that something was wrong. He said to me that Bagle was not well, in fact she was very ill.

"What has happened?" I asked.

"Well", he said, "somehow or other some wheat had spilled out of the storage shed, and Bagle had eaten a large quantity of it." The wheat had swelled up in her stomach and had damaged her kidneys and was also poisoning her whole system.

Everything possible was done for Bagle, and no expense was spared but sadly to no avail, too much wheat had been consumed and Bagle was put to sleep to save her from any further suffering. Fred himself was very upset, and Sarah and Helen were devastated, as were the whole family for many days. I myself shed a few tears, as she was such a wonderful pony, so kind and good-natured.

My mind went back fifty-two years to a decision I had to make regarding my Dad's old pony named 'Peg'. Life can be very cruel sometimes, but time is a great healer.

Sarah and Helen have a new pony now, but I know in their heart of hearts they will never forget Bagle, the first pony they ever had.

Bagle

158

A small selection of the many Letters I have received over the years

2nd March, 1984

Dear Mr. Strange,

I am enclosing a complimentary copy of the Spring issue of our magazine, in which you will see in our Postbox columns (page 65) an item referring to the award of a Silver Cross of St. George.

This Cross, hallmarked in sterling silver, cannot be purchased and is only awarded to those who make an outstanding contribution to furthering the English way of life.

I am pleased to say that you have been mentioned by our readers for this Award which I feel to be amply justified. It is being sent under separate cover, and I hope that you will wear it with pride as a small token of our appreciation of your valiant efforts.

ROY FAIERS, *Editor of 'This England'.*

20 March, 1991

Dear Alf,

Your talk and demonstration was undoubtedly the highlight of the recent TIC Familiarisation Tour!

Many thanks for giving us your time and skills. All the staff were very enthusiastic and I'm sure they will treasure the memory, repeat your stories and suggest a visit to "Alf Strange", to their visitors.

Thank you so much. Best wishes.

INGRID J. JONES, TDAP Manager, Shropshire

Dear Uncle Alf,

My folks sent me a copy of your book, and I wanted to be sure to write to tell you how much I enjoyed it – I doubt I ever sat down and read a book with so much enjoyment.

Sitting here in the Arizona desert, I found myself (for about the first time since I reached this spectacular land) homesick for all the green fields of England, and particularly all the charm and beauty I was lucky enough to see as a child growing up in Shropshire.

Thank you for all the wonderful stories you recounted of the brothers and Frankton, and especially for a look at my grandfather whom I've always regretted never having known.

I'd never wish a coronary problem on anyone, but if it gave you the impetus to write this beautiful book, I guess it did do something good. I hope your health continues as good as the humour was in your stories. Give my regards to my Auntie Vera, my cousins, and of course my Uncle Jack.

Love, SIMON   (*Tucson, Arizona*)

15 April, 1996

Dear Mr. Strange,

I visited England in January with Dave Duckett. You no doubt knew him when he had Peplow Forge. We have become great friends since his move to the U.S. While visiting his father, Larry Pritchard, I saw copies of your three books. On return home, I ordered them from Gee & Son.

I must tell you that I devoured all three in very short time. You see, I have shod horses for 49 years, and can readily identified with many of your experiences. You have a wonderful way of relating each story.

It is ironic, that you lost all those cattle from hoof and mouth disease, and now the plague of today's disease of cattle in your country. Truly, a disaster that doesn't need a repeat.

I hope you are working on book number four. But, I just wanted to drop a line to tell you how much I enjoyed the books.

BILL MILLER

August 15, 1995

Dear Alf,

Just a short letter to say how pleased dad and I were to finally see you working in the 'Blacksmith's Shop.' We certainly had a pleasant day, with the lovely weather and a trip on the canal at Llangollen.

Thank you for letting me borrow the newspaper cutting, as you can see I have enclosed the original together with two photocopies.

As I mentioned to you last week I enjoy working with computers and so I have attached a poster that I have designed for you, you may find it useful. Also, I hope you enjoy my poem, which might make you smile and help you to remember the day.

I do hope my letter finds you and your family well, who knows we may meet again.

Kind regards,

SUSAN A. PRESCOTT and PETER PARKINSON HUGHES

A TRIP DOWN MEMORY LANE

The old folks travelled from Lancs down to Shropshire,
On the way we passed cornfields ascore.
We're not used to the countryside scene here,
Its a sight Tyldesley's not famous for.

We stopped at Brow Farm at Welsh Frankton,
Alf and Vera made us some tea.
We took our brew into the garden,
And sat on a pew by a tree.

Alf showed us his skill as a blacksmith,
A horseshoe and poker were made.
As our driver pumped hard on the bellows,
The heat from the glow made him fade.

As Alf worked he told us his stories,
And recalled a tale of his gran.
How she'd sit on the anvil to test it,
But she ended by burning her bum!

161

The pot with a lid was a treasure,
You couldn't buy one like it today.
But I don't fancy any rice pudding,
Since hearing Alf's tale t'other day.

The visit was very nostalgic,
For my dad used to come as a lad,
To spend time with his father's Aunt Annie,
It was th'only holiday young Peter had.

Alf's gran and my father's were sisters,
From Hengoed Annie and Mary came.
The church no longer remains there,
But City Road still looks the same.

Alf's got a lot going for him,
He writes, is amusing and sharp.
I wish him well in his ventures.
It was a really interesting talk.

CHERNOBYL CHILDREN LIFE LINE

10th October, 1997

Dear Mr. & Mrs. Strange,

Thank you so much for the super demonstration you gave to the children. They thoroughly enjoyed their day out and were delighted to be able to get together and speak their own language for the first time since they arrived, especially in such a delightful spot.

All in all, the children had a marvellous month and were thrilled with all that they were able to see and do, and delighted by all that they were given. These holidays are invaluable for the children, so our heartfelt thanks for your generosity that helped to make this time so special and memorable for so many children.

CORINNE CHIDLEY *(Telford Link)*

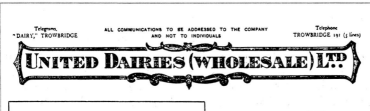

Telegrams,
"DAIRY," TROWBRIDGE

ALL COMMUNICATIONS TO BE ADDRESSED TO THE COMPANY
AND NOT TO INDIVIDUALS

Telephone
TROWBRIDGE 191 (5 lines)

UNITED DAIRIES (WHOLESALE) LTD.

Mr. Thomas Davies,
1 Higher Ridge

Head Office:
TROWBRIDGE,
WILTS.

L.M

10th October, 1931.

Dear Sir(s),

MANUFACTURING MILK PRICE.

The October Manufacturing milk price has already been announced as 4½d. per imperial gallon. With the change in the general conditions, it is anticipated that cheese prices will shew an improvement, and it has been decided that the monthly Manufacturing Milk price payable by United Dairies (Wholesale) Ltd. shall be based as per clause 3 of their contract, namely, on the average wholesale price per lb. of Canadian and New Zealand cheese for the current month instead of being ascertained on the previous month as allowed for in the National contract.

This will definitely be an advantage to you during the present month.

Yours truly,
UNITED DAIRIES (Wholesale) LIMITED.

Managing Director.

Note the price of milk – 4½d. per gallon.

Given to the author by Mrs. Dilys Dyke, granddaughter of Thomas Davies, and mother of Colin and Graham Dyke of J. C. Dykes Supplies of Oswestry, Ellesmere and surrounding districts.

May 14th, 1998

Dear Alf,

The members of the above group wish me to express our gratitude to you all there for making our visit to the Smithy so very enjoyable. We all thoroughly enjoyed the demonstration together with your lovely stories and "sense of humour". Please thank the rest of the team for their welcome with the tea/coffee and tour of the museum. It is gratifying to know that we can still "step back in time" in this modern world. Keep going now Alfie and we hope we shall be able to visit you again in the future.

Kindest regards on behalf of the whole group.

EILWEN J. DEWSLIP
(Secretary St. Anne's Church Fellowship)

17th September, 1999

Dear Alf,

The members of the South Shropshire Visually Impaired Club have asked me to tell you how much they enjoyed their visit to your smithy, it brought back many memories.

We would also like to say how much we appreciated the help and consideration we received from you and your family.

With many thanks, and in the hope that we may visit you again in the not too distant future.

GEORGE JONES

Rose Cottage,
Little Common,
St. Martins,
Oswestry SY11 3HB

Dear Mr. Strange,

My family and I were on holiday recently in the Forest of Dean, when 100´ underground at some Ancient Iron mines I noticed the enclosed epitaph.

Being an avid reader of your books, I thought you may be interested in reading about a fellow namesake (maybe distant relation).

Keep up the good work, but I must say when your books are published not much housework gets done here.

Kindest regards and good health for the future,

SUSAN TALBOT

My Sledge and Anvil lay declined
My bellows too have lost their wind
My fires extinct, my forge decayed.
And in the dust my vice is laid.
My coals are spent, My irons gone
My nails are drove
My work is done.

The Epitaph above is to a blacksmith named William Strange who passed away on the 6th Juine 1746 and was laid to rest in Nettlebed Churchyard.

It is now copied out and stands as a tribute to blacksmiths working underground in the Ancient Iron Mines at

Clearwell Caves
Coleford,
Royal Forest of Dean,
Gloucestershire,
GL16 8JR.

The final chapter

In my final summing up of my fourth book and when looking back to the first time I put pen to paper which was about 23 years ago, I little thought then that I would achieve my life long ambition of recording the history of my little village and its characters for the last 100 years or so. For someone who has only moved house once in 75 years, and that was only about 100 yards, also I have never been abroad yet I have probably met people from every nation in the world.

Blacksmiths and farming are very closely connected. I remember the twenties when farming was in disarray. I have seen farming have its ups and downs but I can honestly say that farming is now going through the worst recession in my lifetime. Agriculture is one of the biggest industries in the country, when the farmer is doing well the countryside is doing well and there is no better spender than the farmer. But at the moment he is not allowed to play on a level field, a new phrase that has recently been brought out.

Yes, there may well be some wealthy farmers whose grandfathers bought his farm in the 1920's or 1930's and it has been handed down through the various generations, not a lot of overheads. Whilst his neighbour may have only bought his farm in the last 20 or 30 years, no comparison in the outgoing of the two farms.

Where I live on the main road I don't see as many new tractors and new farm vehicles going to Oswestry and various implement dealers another industry that employs a lot of labour.

An old country saying is 'it is suprising how many people make a living out of the old cow', and 'never judge a man by the clothes he wears !' A tip I give to young people in business is, don't think for one minute that every new car that visits your farmyard or place of business is paid for. Probably their mortgage is bigger than yours and their bank overdraft as well.

I think if I were lucky enough to have my life over again I would TELL my bank manager what my plans were and what overdraft I require, not ASK him. That is if there are any bank managers left to talk to in our fast, high finance, changing world. Remember if the banks and building societies did not lend money to the general public what price their job. I think that my age group has probably had the best of this world.

Those days when a man's word was his bond, and the shake of a hand could clinch any deal, and when a 2 o'clock appointment meant 2 o'clock not 2.45 p.m. or even later are long gone.

I will now finish my final writing with many thanks for all the thousands of letters I have received, also to my family for being so helpful and have accepted my changing moods when my writing was not going so well. A big Thank-you to the thousands of you who have bought my books helping me to raise lots of money for my chosen charity the Coronary Care Unit at The Royal Shrewsbury Hospital, and to Ward 24 I would like to say a special Thank-you.

I Love You All.

Thanks,
ALF.

SATURDAY 25th MARCH 2000.